SCIENCE
in the Creation Week

Content and "Hands-on" Science Skills Curriculum Grades 2-5

One Year Science Curriculum
(Can be repeated at three separate skill levels)

by David Unfred, MSc, MBA
Illustrated by Nathanael Long

Noble Publishing Associates
Gresham, OR 97030

Noble Publishing Associates, the publishing arm of Christian Life Workshops, is an association of Christian authors dedicated to serving God and assisting one another in the production, promotion, and distribution of audio, video, and print publications. For instructions on how you may participate in our association, or for information about our complete line of materials write to:

Noble Press Associates
P.O. Box 2250
Gresham, Oregon 97030

or call (503) 667-3942.

© 1994 by
David Unfred, MSc, MBA

Science in the Creation Week
Content and "Hands-on" Science Skills Curriculum
First Printing - May, 1991
Second Printing - August 1991
Third Printing - Revised and Expanded Edition - January, 1992
Fourth Printing - May, 1994

ISBN: 1-56857-006-6

Printed in the United States of America.

About the Author

From a commitment to integrating science education and Biblical truth, *Science in the Creation Week* was born.

Dave Unfred has taught at Christian Heritage College in San Diego, the Institute for Creation Research's Graduate School, and Wayland Baptist University. He was a member of the curriculum development team that produced the outstanding **Good Science K-6 Curriculum** and is listed as its editor. Other educational materials by David Unfred include **Dinosaurs and the Bible** (1990, Huntington House Publishing), **The Great Dinosaur Adventure Game** (1988, Master Books), **Mystery of Early Man and the Bible** (in press), and **When Angels Sing** (in press).

While teaching hands-on science to his own daughters, and other home school and Christian school students, Dave discovered a need for more science content. What better way to provide this content than to take science back to where it began-- Creation Week!

About the Illustrator

Nathanael Long (age 13) has been drawing since he was five. Home schooled for the past four years, he has either placed or won in numerous national contests for young artists. Nat even developed his own comic strip, which he sold as a serial to friends, when he was ten.

It has been the Author's privilege to work with a young man so dedicated to serving the Lord with his skill.

Why *Science in the Creation Week* ?

Grades 2 through 5 are an excellent opportunity for science education. But too often students (and teachers) are discouraged, and grow to fear or dislike science. Why? One reason is the misconception that science is memorizing endless terms, principles and laws. How should we teach science? Before answering this question, let's be clear on what science is.

If you were going to produce a championship basketball team, the first thing you would do is have the potential players study the rules. After numerous tests and memory drills, you would give a Final Exam. You are ready to select your championship team--who obviously will be the five players that scored highest on the exam. Absurd! Instead you would develop individual player skills with repeated drills. Rules are important, but if a kid knows the rule book by heart and can't dribble or shoot, he won't make this championship team.

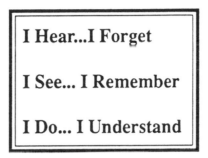

I Hear...I Forget

I See... I Remember

I Do... I Understand

Science is a process that uses **science skills** to explore Creation. Just as our imaginary team requires athletic skills, a student of science requires skills that enable **discovery, inquiry,** and **curiosity.** What are these science skills? They are skills such as observing, measuring, predicting, developing hypotheses, making models, communicating results--in other words **science must be hands-on!** (Refer to the Science Skills Index of the "Contents/ Scope and Sequence.").

Science in the Creation Week provides the student with both science content and hands-on discovery activities. In the Elementary grades science education should develop science skills. These skills will provide a framework onto which the student can build an operational vocabulary--not just memorized words, but a foundation to understand the concepts, principles and laws of science.

How is *Science in the Creation Week* Used?

Science in the Creation Week has a unique Scope and Sequence--a **logical progression of activities that builds** the student's curiosity, confidence, and, of course, his science skills. A good hands-on science curriculum (as opposed to a book of science experiments) challenges him to move forward from the simple to the complex.

To distinguish between activities of differing levels of skill and science content, three characters are used. They are the Explorer, the Investigator, and the Researcher. Just as each student is unique, so are our three characters. The difficulty level increases from Explorer to Reseacher, as do the demands for critical thinking and science skills. These characters also help each student quickly identify activities within his capability--and continually challenge him to move on to the more difficult activities. Sometimes these three characters even provide a little humor.

Explorer Level. This level best corresponds to Grades 2 and 3. Unit One, dealing with the five senses, is almost wholly designed for the Explorer Level. Experience shows that these grade levels have students showing the greatest diversity in science skills. **Science in the Creation Week** has the advantage of letting the student choose the next level that will challenge!

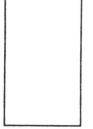

Investigator Level. These activites are demonstrating concepts and principles to a greater extent than the Explorer Level--approximately corresponding to Grades 3 and 4. In a traditional textbook approach, this is where students begin to loose their affection for science. Uniquely, **Science in the Creation Week** focuses the student on all major areas of science, but in a way that concepts are built upon each other.

Researcher Level. In addition to a larger operational vocabulary, the student working at this level has a greater opportunity to develop hypotheses and models. Most of the activities will challenge the student to use experimental design and more effectively communicate data using graphs, tables, and even some statistical analyses. *Science in the Creation Week* **provides both science content and science skill development.** And what better way to study science than to start with the Creation Week--where it all began!

What Do I Need to Do *Science in the Creation Week* ?

One of the problems with other science process skill curricula is the **preparation time** and **equipment needed** to do the activities. *Science in the Creation Week* minimizes preparation time. In addition, the outstanding discovery activities were specifically developed around materials that are commonly used or even discarded at home! If necessary, all materials for these activities can be purchased through hardware supply and grocery stores.

Do I Need A Science Background To Teach This Curriculum?

No! The Teacher Guidelines provide a general introduction to the operational vocabulary, concepts, and science skills taught in <u>each</u> activity. **Focus questions** that guide the student's inquiry and responses are highlighted in quotation marks and bold type. Student data recording sheets are provided. **And, the "Contents/Scope and Sequence" section helps the teacher plan each activity by showing the time required to prepare, as well as, complete each activity.**

CONTENTS/ SCOPE and SEQUENCE

Activity	LEVEL	Science Skills Index												Time		
		Observing	Classifying	Predicting	Experimenting	Communicating	Illustrating	Recording Data	Designing	Calculating	Making Models	Creat. Writing	Using Ref. Matl	Prep. (min.)	Act. (min).	Page #
UNIT ONE: Human Senses																
God Made the Sense of Taste	E	X	X	X	X	X		X						20	20	3
God Made the Sense of Touch	E	X	X	X	X	X								10	20	4
God Made the Sense of Smell	E	X	X	X	X	X								20	15	4
God Made the Sense of Hearing	E	X	X	X	X	X			X		X			10	15	7
God Made the Sense of Sight	E	X	X	X	X	X		X	X					20	15	7
Science Tools and Our Senses	I	X	X	X									X	0	15	9
UNIT TWO: Light, Energy, and Matter																
Light Travels in a Straight Line	E	X			X	X	X		X					20	20	13
Focused Light Produces Heat	E	X			X	X								10	15	14
Matter: The Stuff of Creation	E	X	X	X		X								20	20	15
Absorbed Light Produces Energy	I	X			X	X	X		X					20	45	16
Sunlight: Light of Many Colors	I	X	X		X	X	X	X						20	40	16
Property of Matter: Gravity	I	X			X	X	X				X			20	40	18
Design in Matter and Gravity	I	X			X	X	X		X		X			20	30	19
Matter and Energy Interact	I	X	X	X	X	X								10	20	20
Design of Interacting Systems	I	X	X	X	X	X			X		X			15	25	21
Light and Wavelenghts	R	X	X		X	X	X	X	X	X	X			15	15	22
Light and Image Mystery	R	X			X	X	X	X	X					20	40	22
Elements: God's Building Blocks	R	X	X	X		X							X	60	45	24
Light: A Property of Elements	R	X	X	X	X	X					X		X	20	30	26
Electrical Energy in a Closed Sys.	R	X			X	X	X	X	X					20	45	27

E = Explorer Level; **I** = Inspector Level; **R** = Researcher Level; **Prep** (Min) = Time (minutes) to prepare the Activity; **Act** (Min) = Time (minutes) to complete the Activity.

CONTENTS/ SCOPE and SEQUENCE

Science Skills Index   Time

Activity	LEVEL	Observing	Classifying	Predicting	Experimenting	Communicating	Illustrating	Recording Data	Designing	Graphing	Making Models	Creat. Writing	Using Ref. Matl	Prep. (min.)	Act (min).	Page #
UNIT THREE: Water and the Atmosphere																
Water and Measuring Volume	E	X	X	X	X		X							10	30	31
Water Pressure and Depth	E	X	X	X	X	X								10	30	33
Air Occupies Space	E	X		X	X	X			X					10	20	34
Air Has Pressure	E	X		X	X	X			X					10	20	34
Identifying Clouds	E	X	X					X						0	10	35
Making Solutions	I	X	X	X	X	X								15	15	36
How Fast Do Ice Cubes Melt?	I	X	X	X	X	X		X		X	X			20	90	36
Air Pressure and a Vacuum	I	X	X	X	X	X					X			15	30	39
Air and Kinetic Energy	I	X	X	X	X	X			X		X		X	45	30	39
Gases in Air	I	X		X	X	X					X			30	30	41
Atmospheric Systems - Clouds	R	X	X	X	X	X								15	15	43
The Water Cycle Model	R	X					X				X			0	30	44
Measuring Relative Humidity	R	X	X		X			X		X			X	45	30	45
Air, Water, Vibration, and Sound	R	X	X	X	X	X		X	X		X			30	45	47
Newton's Third Law Races	R	X	X	X	X	X			X					30	45	48
Testing for Gases in Atmosphere	R	X	X	X	X	X		X		X				20	60	49
Testing Water Quality	R	X	X	X	X	X		X	X	X				30	45	50

E = Explorer Level; **I** = Inspector Level; **R** = Researcher Level; **Prep** (Min) = Time (minutes) to prepare the Activity; **Act** (Min) = Time (minutes) to complete the Activity.

CONTENTS/ SCOPE and SEQUENCE

Science Skills Index — Time

Activity	LEVEL	Observing	Classifying	Predicting	Experimenting	Communicating	Illustrating	Recording Data	Designing	Graphing	Making Models	Creat. Writing	Using Ref. Matl	Prep. (min.)	Act. (min).	Page #
UNIT FOUR: Land and Plants																
Minerals in the Bible	E	X	X		X	X								20	30	55
Rocks: God's Building Blocks	E	X	X			X							X	10	40	56
Making Soil From Rocks	E	X	X	X	X	X					X			10	40	56
God Made Plants to Reproduce	E	X			X	X								20	20	57
Plants Interact With Soil	E	X			X	X								30	15	59
Property of Hardness in Minerals	I	X	X					X					X	10	30	61
Where Rocks Are Found	I	X	X		X		X						X	15	45	61
Plants Interact With Atmosphere	I	X		X	X	X								20	30	63
How Plants Interact With Light	I	X	X	X	X	X		X	X					20	30	47
Plants and Electrical Energy	I	X		X	X	X					X			15	20	66
God's Design in Minerals	R	X	X	X	X	X	X	X	X		X			20	45	67
Acids and Bases	R	X	X	X	X	X		X	X		X			20	60	68
Chemical Cannons	R	X	X	X	X	X					X		X	20	45	69
Seeds and Energy	R	X	X	X	X	X		X	X	X				20	50	70
Separating Plant Leaf Pigments	R	X	X	X	X	X		X	X					20	60	72
Soil Environments	R	X	X	X	X	X		X	X	X	X		X	30	60	73
UNIT FIVE: Sun, Moon and Stars																
God Made and Named the Stars	E	X	X		X	X					X			30	30	77
Phases of the Moon	E	X	X		X	X	X	X			X			30	60	80
Using the Sun to Tell Time	E	X	X	X	X	X	X	X	X					30	40	81
What Causes the Seasons	E	X			X	X	X				X			20	30	81

E = Explorer Level; **I** = Inspector Level; **R** = Researcher Level; **Prep** (Min) = Time (minutes) to prepare the Activity; **Act** (Min) = Time (minutes) to complete the Activity.

CONTENTS/ SCOPE and SEQUENCE

Science Skills Index   Time

Activity	LEVEL	Observing	Classifying	Predicting	Experimenting	Communicating	Illustrating	Recording Data	Designing	Graphing	Making Models	Creat. Writing	Using Ref. Matl	Prep. (min.)	Act. (min.)	Page #
UNIT FIVE: Continued																
Relative Motion of the Stars	I	X	X	X	X	X		X	X	X	X			20	60	83
Locating Constellations	I	X			X	X							X	0	60	84
Model of the Earth, Sun and Moon	I	X	X	X	X	X					X			20	20	86
Making and Using a Telescope	R	X	X		X	X					X	X	X	40	90+	87
Studying Sunspots	R	X	X		X	X	X	X						20	30	89
Studying the "Greenhouse" Effect	R	X	X	X	X	X			X	X	X			20	60	90
UNIT SIX: Birds and Sealife																
Animals That Fly	E	X	X			X	X							20	20	97
Animals That Live in Water	E	X	X			X	X							20	20	98
When Noah Went Fishing	E	X	X				X				X	X	X	30	30	98
What Do Birds Like to Eat?	I	X	X	X	X	X			X					25	30	101
What Do Birds Use for Nests?	I	X	X	X	X	X			X					10	45	101
Making an Aquatic Environment	I	X	X	X	X	X	X		X					20	60	102
Embryo Development	R	X	X	X	X	X	X		X		X		X	60	120	104
Changes in Aquatic Community	R	X	X	X	X	X	X	X	X		X			60	60	106
Dissecting a Fish	R	X	X	X		X	X						X	30	90	107
Dissecting a Bird	R	X	X	X		X	X						X	30	90	109
Studying Decomposers and Fossils	R	X	X	X	X	X			X					30	30	111
UNIT SEVEN: Land Animals and Humans																
God Made the Dinosaurs	E	X		X		X					X			20	20	115
Observing Animals in a Terrarium	E	X	X	X	X	X	X	X			X			60	120	116

E = Explorer Level; **I** = Inspector Level; **R** = Researcher Level; **Prep** (Min) = Time (minutes) to prepare the Activity; **Act** (Min) = Time (minutes) to complete the Activity.

CONTENTS/ SCOPE and SEQUENCE

E = Explorer Level; **I** = Inspector Level; **R** = Researcher Level; **Prep** (Min) = Time (minutes) to prepare the Activity; **Act** (Min) = Time (minutes) to complete the Activity.

Using Our Senses to Explore God's Creation

Since the creation of the world His invisible attributes, His eternal power and divine nature, have been clearly seen, being understood through what has been made....
Romans 1:18.

Using Our Senses to Explore God's Creation

**EXPLORER
LEVEL**

Learning Objectives. The student will:--
* Classify and describe objects by using the five senses;
* Record responses using a variety of charts and tables;
* Evaluate, compare objects, and make predictions using the senses;
* Suggest ways to test objects using the senses;
* Recognize some ways that senses are helped by tools of science.

Teacher Guidelines. The activities in this Unit will require either group interaction between students or interaction between the teacher and individual student. Activities are organized for one sense to be investigated during each class period.

Materials Preparation

Sense of Taste Activities: Labelled foods for a Taste Center- dill pickle, lemon, potato chip, peanut butter, vegetable shortening (solid), bitter chocolate, orange peel, sweet chocolate, apple, onion (substitutions allowed); blindfold.

Sense of Touch Activities: Dark pillow case or other bag that cannot be seen through; 3 common, harmless "mystery" objects that can be identified, at varying levels of difficulty, by touch.

Sense of Smell Activities: Five plastic or paper cups; blindfold; variety of spices or foods with distinctive odors in each labeled cup; unknown (one of the spices or/foods in a cup labeled "unknown").

Sense of Hearing Activities: Small box that cannot be seen through; 3 objects of different shapes and weights that move freely inside the box-one object should be attracted to a magnet (optional). Supplemental Activity: Tape recorder and audio tape recording of different common sounds.

Sense of Hearing Activities: Small box that cannot be seen through; 3 objects of different shapes and weights that move freely inside the box-one object should be attracted to a magnet (optional). Supplemental Activity: Tape recorder and audio tape recording of different common sounds.

Sense of Sight Activities. Ruler (in inches); white poster board that the student can cut into 8 one-half inch by two inch strips; red, blue, green, yellow, brown, orange, purple crayons or coloring pens; have the student color each strip a different color (leave one strip white on both sides); a green, empty plastic bottle with half inch opening (2-liter soft drink bottles are ideal); different colored glass or plastic through which the student can view the colored strips (optional).

Activities

God made humans with five senses. As each student investigates these senses, he or she should think of answers to this question, **"Why did God give us these five senses?".**

Activity One - **God Made the Sense of Taste.**

There are four basic tastes: Sour (like a lemon); Salty; Bitter (like an orange peel); and Sweet. Have the student taste each of the foods in the Taste Center. The student will **classify** these foods by the property of taste and write the name of the food in a box below the appropriate taste. Have the student **evaluate** each of the four basic tastes (whether "yum", "yuk", or "take it or leave it") by placing an "X" in the box across from the appropriate "face" symbol. The student can record this data on page 5.

Now repeat the taste classification with the student blindfolded and holding his or her nose. The student (helped by the teacher or another student) will record the new information on the bottom of page 5.

The student can now compare the two sets of data. **"Is there any difference?"** **"If so, what is different?"**

Activity Two - God Made the Sense of Touch.

Have the student sit in a chair. The student places one bare foot into a bag containing the mystery objects. **"How many objects are in the bag?"**.

Next have the student describe the objects' properties. As the student describes the properties of each object (smooth, round, hard, soft, etc.), the teacher can record the responses on the Data Record Sheet, page 6, or on the blackboard.

After each object is described the student should predict what the object is. *Do not remove the objects from or allow the student to look into the bag.*

Next, the student repeats the activity using his or her fingers. Again, the teacher may record the observations and predictions on chart, page 6. Have the student compare both sets of data. Let the student suggest what the data means about the sense of touch with feet and touch with fingers.

Activity Three - God Made the Sense of Smell

Let the student examine each labeled cup with the sense of smell. The student should be encouraged to describe the properties of smell. The cup with one of the same foods or spices, labeled "unknown," should be hidden from the student at this time.

Next, the student is blindfolded. Now have the student smell the cup with the unknown. The student may be allowed to compare the unknown with all of the "known" sample cups while remaining blindfolded. The teacher (or another student) can call out the name of each known sample as the blindfolded student examines the samples using only the sense of smell.

After predicting, the student may remove the blindfold. Was the unknown identified? (It may be fun for the students to prepare another unknown for the blindfolded teacher to identify!).

God Made the Sense of Taste

	SOUR	SALTY	BITTER	SWEET
🙂				
😐				
☹️				

	SOUR	SALTY	BITTER	SWEET
	_____	_____	_____	_____
	_____	_____	_____	_____
	_____	_____	_____	_____
	_____	_____	_____	_____
With Blind-fold and Holding Nose	_____	_____	_____	_____
	_____	_____	_____	_____
	_____	_____	_____	_____
	_____	_____	_____	_____

God Made the Sense of Touch

(What if our feet were hands?)

	Properties	Prediction
First Un-known Object		
Second Unknown Object		
Third Un-known Object		

(With hands)

	Properties	Prediction
First Unknown Object		
Second Unknown Object		
Third Unknown Object		

Activity Four - **God Made the Sense of Hearing**

This activity is best done with a group of students. The teacher first shows the students the "mystery" box and asks the students what is in the box? Next, ask how would they find out what is in the box--remind them that the box cannot be opened. When "shaking the box" is suggested, shake the box fast and then slowly tilt the box. Ask the students if they hear any difference. **"How many objects are in the box?"**

You may at this time expand this activity by asking what objects are in the "mystery" box. **"Is there any way we can find out more information about the objects in the box?"**

If you have a magnet, ask the students how this can be used to help find out more about properties of the objects in the box. Let the students use the magnet with the box to investigate the "mystery" box. At the end of class ask for a final prediction about the contents of the "mystery" box and open the box.

Supplemental Activity. The sense of hearing can be investigated by recording various sounds on a audio tape recorder. Listening to the recording, the student tries to predict what made the sounds. (It may be possible for one group of students to make the recording for another group to identify.).

Activity Five - **God Made the Sense of Sight**

The student begins this activity by making colored (both sides) poster board strips. Have the student fill in the chart (page 8) with the color name of each strip. (If necessary, a color vocabulary can be written on blackboard.).

The teacher or another student will place all of the colored strips into the see-through, green plastic container. Seal the container. The student now views the strips in the container. **"Has the color of the strips changed?" "Has the color of all of the strips changed?" "Which is the red strip, etc.?"**

The student may repeat this activity using differently colored see-through glass or plastic as available.

What would the world have looked like, if God had only made "green" sunlight?

God Made the Sense of Sight

Chart

COLOR OF STRIP (Color the Box)						
NAME OF COLOR						
COLOR IN GREEN LIGHT						

**INVESTIGATOR
LEVEL**

***Activity Six* - Science Tools and Our Senses**

Page 10 is a chart of "tools" used by scientists to research God's Creation. The student writes the name(s) of the human sense(s) that the tool enhances. If the science tool is not familiar to the student, use of the dictionary or encyclopedia. The teacher can emphasize that a scientist needs tools to do his or her work--just as a carpenter needs hammers or a mechanic needs screw drivers and wrenches. Follow-on questions could include a discussion or class project about tools that are used by people to do different kinds of work.

Ask questions such as **"Why do scientists need tools?".** (On the chart, the pH Meter measures properties in foods that can affect taste--acid foods are usually sour. The Analytical Balance accurately measures weight --enhancing the senses of sight and touch.).

NOTES

Science Tool	Senses Helped
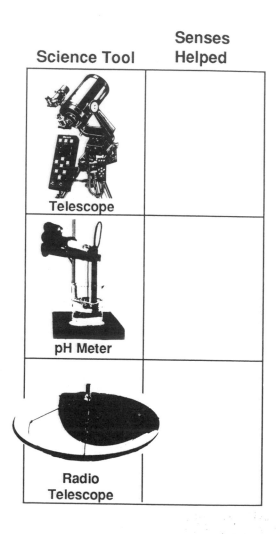 Microscope	
Analytical Balance	
Electron Microscope	

Science Tool	Senses Helped
Telescope	
pH Meter	
Radio Telescope	

Question. **Which of the five human senses can these science tools help?**

UNIT TWO

Light, Energy, and Matter
Day One of Creation

Then God said, "Let there be light", and there was light. And God called the light day, and the darkness He called night. And there was evening and there was morning, the first day. **Genesis 1:3, 5**

God Created Light, Energy, and Matter

Learning Objectives

Explorer Level. The student will: -
* Recognize that God created light and energy;
* Conduct experiments to discover different properties of light;
* Observe that light travels in a straight line and interacts with a mirror system;
* Conduct experiments to show that light can be changed to heat energy;
* Observe that matter exists and its properties.

Investigator Level. The student will: -

* Observe that light can be focused and absorbed;
* Demonstrate, by interaction with water, that sunlight is composed of differently colored lights;
* Observe and demonstrate the Law of Conservation of Energy and Matter;
* Observe and demonstrate how gravity interacts with matter;
* Conduct an experiment showing how design helps matter interact with gravity;
* Conduct an experiment to demonstrate an open and closed electrical system.

Researcher Level. The student will: -
* Make inferences of how fiber optics works by observing properties of light;
* Develop a model of how a solar oven works using observations of properties of light;
* Recognize a basic concept in the Wave Theory of Light;
* Understand that matter is made of the elements;
* Demonstrate that light is a property of elements;
* Show how electrical charges travel over circuits in closed systems.

Materials Preparation

Explorer Level Activities. One flashlight; four 6" by 8" stiff poster board rectangles, each with a one and one-half inch circle cut in the center-- Students can use a bottle opening of approximately this size, or take this opportunity to use a compass to draw the circle cut-out; two hand-held mirrors (make-up or compact mirrors will work); four books of approximately the same height that can be made to stand on end; magnifier; black and white construction paper.

Investigator Level Activities. Several colors of construction paper; shallow pan; ice cubes; mirror; crayons or markers that represent the colors of a rainbow; two heavy balls of different sizes; pencil, potato, and fork; shallow dish, paper, and matches; flashlight battery, flashlight bulb, and electrical wire (2 three inch pieces).

Researcher Level Activities. Empty Pringles potato chip canister, flashlight, waxed paper; fifty 3" x 5" cards or pieces of paper; shallow dish, matches, table salt, and methanol; red colored paper, dark colored construction paper, aluminum foil, tape, and battery-bulb-wire system above.

Teacher Guidelines and Activities

**EXPLORER
LEVEL**

Activity One - **Property of Light: Light Travels in a Straight Line.**

"Can light travel around corners?" "Does light only travel in a straight line?". Position the circles cut in poster board in a straight line as shown on page 14. In a darkened room, the student holds a flashlight next to the circular hole in the poster board. Have the student observe the light projected on a wall and trace its outline on a sheet of paper (the closer to the wall the smaller the circle projected). Next, move one of the middle circles straight up until half the hole is blocked. Shine the flashlight through the series as before and have the student trace the projection on the wall. **"What is different?" "Is light blocked when solid paper is put in the light's path?" "Does this experiment show that light travels in a straight line?" "Does light 'flow' around objects in its path.?"** (Diagram One, page 14).

"If light travels in a straight line, is it possible to bend light?"
"How could you make light change directions?"
Using the set-up in *Activity One* , the student holds a mirror at the end of the series of circles. Have the student move the mirror at different angles in the darkened room. What happens to the light projection?

Diagram One

Activity Two - **Property of Light: Focused Light Produces Heat Energy.**
Using a magnifier, focus sunlight on a sheet of black construction paper. The student observes changes that occur where the light is focused on the paper. CAUTION: Focused light will burn skin! Activity should be adult supervised.
"Energy is the power to cause change. What change has the focused light produced on the black construction paper?"

Activity Three - **Matter: The Stuff of Creation**

God made light and matter on the first day of Creation. Matter is what everything we see or feel is made from. Matter may be hard, like a chair, floor, or a rock. Matter may be soft, like Jello or skin. Matter may be invisible, like wind. Or matter may be wet, like water.

Have the student identify and classify as many properties of matter as time permits. As a class activity, each student can contribute to a list on a blackboard or a poster size sheet of paper.

Example.

Matter	Properties
Pencil	Surface has different hardness (eraser, wood, pencil graphite); surface has different feel (texture); different colors on surface.
Apple	Thin, smooth, hard surface; surface skin is red with small black dots; fingernail can cut surface; not perfectly round; black stem on one end with small, dry leaf-like *structures* on the opposite side.

Note: One way to develop observation skills is to continue to ask "What other properties can you see?". As the student continues to look at an object, the more exacting the observations become. Allow the students to use their own vocabulary. Also, as the teacher, you can introduce vocabulary words, such as *propertry* or *structure* , used in the context of the descriptions being provided by the students.

**INVESTIGATOR
LEVEL**

Activity Four **- Property of Light: Absorbed Light
Produces Heat Energy.**

Fold and staple a piece of white construction
paper into the shape of a box lid--edges of the lid are
about one and one-half inches deep. Repeat the
procedure with black construction paper. In a
shallow pan, place four to six ice cubes and cover
them with the white lid. Cover the same number of
ice cubes with the black lid. Finally, place the same
number of ice cubes together in a tray uncovered.
Put all three trays in the sun.

Every five minutes the student will look under the paper lids. **"Is
there any difference in how fast the ice melts?" "Which set of ice
cubes is melting the fastest?" "Does the color of the paper lid have
any effect on how fast the ice cubes melt?"**

You may want to continue the experiment using differently colored
construction papers. Have the student predict which colors will melt the ice
more quickly.

Activity Five **- Property of Light: Sunlight Is Light Of Many Colors.**

Place a shallow pan of water on a window ledge that receives direct
sunlight (Diagram Two). Have the student place a mirror in the pan of water.
The student moves the mirror until a rainbow (**light spectrum**: red, orange,
yellow, green, blue, and violet) is projected onto the wall. The student can
color the light spectrum below and on the chart, page 17.

Colors of the Light Spectrum

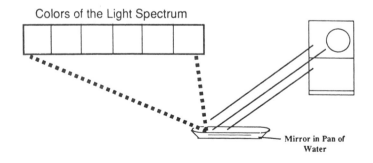

Mirror in Pan of
Water

Diagram Two

Water and cut glass can separate sunlight into different colors. On the chart below color each square a color of the light spectrum as it is reflected onto the wall from the mirror in the pan of water. Color the squares in the order in which they occur in the reflected light spectrum.

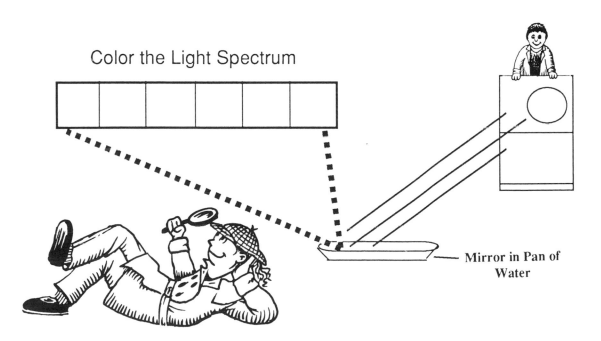

Color the Light Spectrum

Mirror in Pan of Water

The rainbow is a sign of the promise that God made for Noah and all mankind. What was that promise? Do the colors of a rainbow always occur in the same order as your light spectrum above? What has to happen before a rainbow can be seen?

Activity Six - Property of Matter: Gravity.

Have the student drop an object. **"Describe what happened."**
"Why did it happen?"

The *force* that caused the object to fall is **gravity**. Matter has the property of gravity. Because the Earth is large--its property of gravity affects other objects on its surface--such as the object dropped by the student.

In this activity the student investigates how the force of gravity affects two objects. Take two "heavy" balls of different diameters--metal bearings are excellent for this experiment. The two balls of different size must have equally smooth surfaces, and must be heavy enough (though not the same weight) to resist surface friction and air friction. Place the two balls side-by-side at the top of a tilted table or board. The teacher or another student releases the balls at the same time. At the botton of the tilted surface is the "finish-line."

Have the student predict what the outcome will be. The student at the finish-line can then determine if the balls cross at the same time or if one ball was "faster" than the other. Repeat the experiment several times.

Discovery Principle: The force of gravity acts equally on objects--even objects of different sizes.

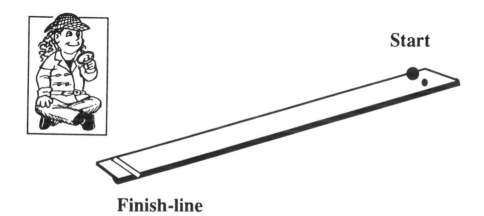

Start

Finish-line

Activity Seven - Design in Matter and Interaction with Gravity.

Design in objects and systems can interact with the force of gravity. For example, a baby spends a lot of time trying to *balance* his ability to stand and walk with the downward pull of gravity.

Stick a pencil through the top half of a potato so that the tip of the pencil barely sticks out the other side (about one-half inch). Have the student experiment with a fork as a *counterweight*. When a proper balance is obtained, the system appears to go against the force of gravity!

Table

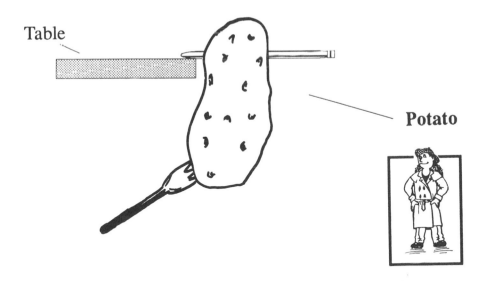

Potato

"What are the different parts that make-up the system above?'

Activity Eight - **Matter and Energy Interact.**

The teacher will set a piece of paper on fire in a shallow dish. As the paper burns have the student describe what is happening.

Matter (the paper) is being changed. Some of the matter is changed to heat and light energy. Some of the matter is changed into smoke and ash.

"Can energy be changed into matter?" Plants use sunlight to build more plant material (*tissue*).

A **law** in science is something that can be shown to be true in Creation all of the time. The **Law of Conservation of Matter and Energy** is that any amount of energy and matter cannot be created or destroyed--only changed into each other. The relationship between energy and matter is stated by the **equation**, $E = mc^2$, or energy equals an amount of matter (mass) times the speed of light squared.

Whether or not you wish to introduce the concept of an equation at this time depends on the experience of the student. The important association is that the paper (matter) is changed into heat and light energy and a different type of matter.

God is not part of His Creation. God made the laws of science and He is not ruled by them. On the first day of Creation, God created both matter and energy, and He made them out of nothing--just by His speaking were matter and energy created!

Activity Nine - **Design of Matter and Energy Systems that Interact.**

The student takes two wires (if coated, make sure a quarter inch of each metal wire end is exposed), a battery, and a light bulb from a flashlight. Give the student the assignment to light the bulb.

When successful, have the student take apart a flashlight. **"How is the flashlight like the battery-wire-light bulb system you designed?"**

When the light bulb is on, the system is closed. When the light bulb is off, the system is open. **Open systems** and **closed systems** are useful concepts that are easily introduced in this activity.

RESEARCHER LEVEL

Activity Ten - **Property: Different Colors Of Light Have Different Wavelengths.**

The chart on page 23, provides an opportunity for the student to develop a basic concept of the Wave Theory of Light. The student will color the spectrum and draw a predicted relative wavelength for each color light. (The drawings should progressively range between the "long" wavelength infrared and the "short" wavelength ultraviolet.). Questions may be asked about the effects of "UV", or the ultraviolet light in sunlight, on human skin. (Major cause of skin cancer.).

Activity Eleven - **A Light and Image Mystery.**

Using an empty Pringles potato chip canister, punch a hole <u>only as large as a pin</u> in the bottom of the canister. Next, place a piece of wax paper over the opposite open-end and secure by a rubber band. In a darkened room, point the pinhole toward a single, open window. Have someone stand outside the window. Look at the image in the waxed paper. Have the student describe what he observes.

Next cut a triangle or letter into a cardboard disk. The disk is large enough to tape over the end of a flashlight so that light only comes through the cut-out. Place the flashlight and potato chip canister on a table in a dark room. The distance from the flashlight to the pinhole should be about the same as the distance of the pinhole from the waxed paper on the potato chip canister. Turn on the flashlight and shine onto the pinhole. Describe the image produced. **What happens when the flashlight is moved closer to the pinhole? What happens when the flashlight is moved away from the pinhole?   Can you solve this mystery?**

Researcher Level Questions: 1. What is the speed of light?   2. What properties of light would you use to make a sun powered oven (solar oven)? 3. Draw a design for a solar oven using these properties of light. 4. Fiber optics is where light is made to travel along a glass fiber. What properties of light could explain why fiber optics works? How is it used?

Chart

How would you describe light? Scientists have imagined that light can be described as waves--something like waves on the ocean. Different colors of light in the **light spectrum** have different **wavelengths**. The red color in the light spectrum, called **infrared**, has the longest wavelength. The opposite end of the spectrum, called **ultraviolet**, has the shortest wavelength.

COLOR SPECTRUM

Infrared					Ultravio-let

DRAW WAVELENGTH

Color each box in the top row to represent the light spectrum. In the bottom row, draw an estimated wavelength line for each color--remember infrared is the longest wavelength and ultraviolet is the shortest (both already drawn).

Activity Twelve - The Elements: God's Building Blocks

The Periodic Table on page 25 lists all of the elements. Everything in Creation is made from at least one, and usually many, of these different elements. Truly, the elements are God's building blocks.

This activity introduces the student to the elements and the basics of atomic theory. Each element on the Periodic Table is a different atom. An atom has three parts: electrons, protons, and neutrons. The protons and neutrons are together in the nucleus. The electrons orbit arount the nucleus. Different elements on the Periodic Table have different numbers of protons, electrons and neutrons. Each kind of element has unique properties because of the number of protons, electrons and neutrons.

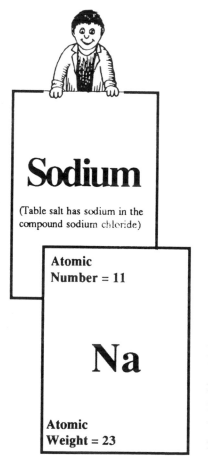

Sodium

(Table salt has sodium in the compound sodium chloride)

Atomic Number = 11

Na

Atomic Weight = 23

Game Rules

A fun way to learn the symbols and names of the elements is to put the symbol on one 3" x 5" card (or piece of paper) and the name of the element on another card. Do this for the first 25 elements (atomic numbers 1 - 25).   Let the student review the Periodic Table before starting the game.   You may want the student to help make the cards. You can also add other information, such as atomic number, atomic weight, and an use of the element. Shuffle the cards (25 symbol and 25 name cards) together. Each student is dealt cards until all cards are distributed among the players. Each player matches the symbol with the name from the cards in his hand. Once the pairs are matched, the player places the pairs on the table in front of him. He is now allowed to draw <u>one</u> card from hand of the player on his right. This process continues until all the pairs are found.   The player with the most matched pairs wins. (In my class winners get awarded by applause from the other players.)

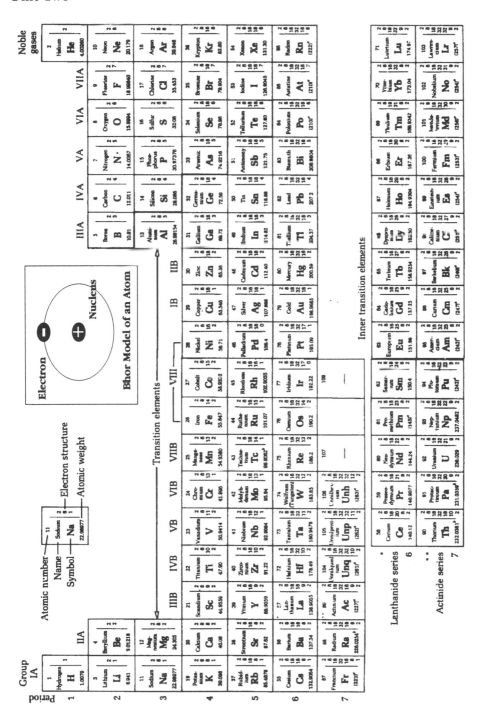

The atomic number of each element represents the number of protons in the nucleus (or the number of orbiting electrons). For example, hydrogen has only one proton, but carbon has six protons in its nucleus. The atomic weight of an element comes from the neutrons plus protons - the more neutrons and protons, the heavier the element is. To find the number of neutrons in an element, subtract the number of protons from the atomic mass and round to the nearest whole number. For example, carbon has 6 protons and 6 neutrons.

Activity Thirteen - **Light: A Property of Elements.**
"Have you ever wondered how a light bulb works?" The wire inside the bulb is heated. Because air has been removed from inside the glass bulb, the wire won't "rust" -- another name for *oxidation* . The wire is made from the element *tungsten* . When the element tungsten is heated, it gives off light.

Requires Adult Supervision!

Elements will give off **different wavelenths**, or colors, of light, when heated. In this activity, the student and teacher will demonstrate this property of elements. Pour *methanol* (available from the pharmacy section of a grocery store) in to a shallow dish. Set the methanol on fire. The flame is a blue color, and almost invisible with lights on--so be careful! Turn off the lights and sprinkle table salt over the flame. The sodium element in the sodium chloride produces an orange light. Hold a red colored piece of paper in the sodium light. **"What color is the paper in sodium light?"** The sodium light makes the red paper appear black.

Other elements can produce different colors. Potassium chloride (Lite Salt) gives a pinkish light. Copper chloride gives a green light. (Some of these elements are part of salts found in chemical fertilizers.) Have the student experiment--with supervision--using different elements. **Make sure that nothing is placed near the flame that is flammable or explosive.**

Researcher Level Question: What element is "burned" in the Sun to produce sunlight? Would a good hypothesis (guess) be that all stars burn the same element to produce starlight? Why?

Activity Fourteen - Interaction of Matter and Electrical Energy in a Closed System.

Elements contain electrical charges. The protons in the nucleus of an atom have a plus (+) or positive electrical charge. The electrons have a minus (-) or negative electrical charge. An element can come together to form a *compound* by sharing the negatively charged electrons with the other elements. When elements come together, the result is called a **chemical compound**. Sodium chloride (table salt) is a chemical compound containing the elements sodium and chlorine. (Find these elements on the Periodic Table on page 25.)

Some chemical compounds can send electrons flowing along a copper wire--not all types of wire allow electrons to travel through them. A flashlight battery produces the electrons that flowed through the wire to make the light bulb come on in Activity Nine--also, did the wire feel warmer?

This activity makes use of an aluminum foil "puzzle" to demonstrate an open and closed system and the flow of electrons.

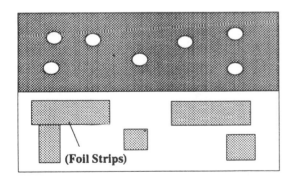

(Foil Strips)

Take a sheet of colored construction paper. Punch holes in one-half of the paper as shown. Paste aluminum foil strips in a pattern shown below. Fold the paper in half lenghtwise so that the side with holes now covers the foil. The foil can be seen throug the hole, but the pattern is hidden.

Using the battery, light bulb and two wires, the student can discover which pairs of holes are connected by the hidden foil. Press the bulb, attached to one wire that is taped to one end of the battery, into the foil of one hole. Press the second wire, attached to the other end of the battery, into the foil of another hole. If the two foil dots are connected, the light comes on--a closed system. After analyzing the puzzle, show the hidden pattern to the student. The student may want to experiment with his own foil patterns. This system is similar to a circuit board and circuit tester.

Who Am I?

(Below are clues from the life of a famous scientist who worked with light, energy, and matter. The scientist's identity is given on bottom of the References, page 132.)

Many scholars say that I am the greatest scientist who ever lived.

I believed in Christ as Savior and in the Bible as God's Word. I wrote many books on Biblical subjects, including a book defending Bishop Ussher's Chronology of the Bible showing that the Creation occurred around 4,000 years before Christ. I believed that God created the world in six literal days and that the "geological record" was mostly a record of the Biblical Flood.

A good scientist is able to observe Creation, and through observation and experimentation, discover laws that God made for the world. Among my scientific achievements, I discovered three laws of motion. I also developed a new branch of mathematics known as The Calculus.

I developed the particle theory of light propagation and did extensive work on the visible spectrum of light. I was also an astronomer and made the first reflecting telescope.

Do you now know who I am? If not, here are a few more clues.

I did much of the ground work for the law of energy conservation. I discovered the law of universal gravitation--shown in cartoons as an apple falling on my head--which never really happened!

Who am I?

(Reference: *Men of Science/Men of God* by H. Morris. 1988.)

UNIT THREE

Water and the Atmosphere
Day Two of Creation

And God made the firmament, and separated the waters which were below the firmament from the waters which were above the firmament. ..And there was evening and there was morning, the second day. Genesis 1:7, 8.

God Created Water and the Atmosphere

Learning Objectives

Explorer Level. The student will: -
* Make volume measurements and comparisons;
* Understand the concept of variability;
* Observe interaction of water pressure and depth;
* Conduct experiment to prove air occupies space;
* Make a system to show that air has the property of pressure;
* Use a barometer;
* Identify cloud types.

Investigator Level. The student will: -
* Experiment with water and solid to form solutions;
* Understand the concept of solubility;
* Experiment with a vacuum;
* Demonstrate and understand that air has kinetic energy using a pinwheel-pulley-color wheel system;
* Observe interaction between primary colors;
* Propose a system for measuring wind speed;
* Develop an understanding of weather maps.

Researcher Level. The student will: -
* Demonstrate cloud formation;
* Based on experimentation, develop and illustrate a model Water Cycle;
* Understand concept of relative humidity;
* Evaluate data using the statistical average.

Materials Preparation

Explorer Level Activities. Eye dropper; rain gauge; large freezer bag; ruler (inches or metric); two clear plastic cups; two 2-liter plastic soft drink bottles.

Investigator Level Activities. Rain gauge; thermometer (Celsius or Fahrenheit); two clear plastic cups; two 2-liter soft drink bottles; ice cubes; sugar cubes; white poster board; colored markers; four plastic gallon milk carton tops; one straw; twine; cardboard, dry ice, candle, large plastic cup.

Researcher Level Activities. Baby food jars (or small jars of equal size), liquid soap; rain guage, steel wool, eye dropper, ruler; plastic straw, balloon, dental floss, tape; wooden board, twine, fishing line or thin wire, nails

Teacher Guidelines and Activities

**EXPLORER
LEVEL**

Activity One - **Water and Measuring Volume.**
The student fills a rain guage to the one-inch mark using an eye dropper. Here is an opportunity to introduce the idea of the *meniscus*.

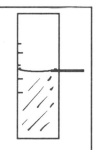

In cylinders, liquids form a curve with the liquid on the side of the cylinder higher than the liquid in the middle. The practice used for measuring liquids, is to measure from the bottom of the curve in middle of the cylinder, called the **meniscus** (*ma-nis'-cuss*).

The student counts the number of drops it takes to reach the one-inch mark. This data is recorded on the data sheet, page 32. Repeat the activity four more times with other students (or at home, with other members of the family), and record their results on the same page. **"Are all the measurements the same?" "What could be some reasons why all the measurements are not the same?"** When measurements of an object or property are not the same, we call this **variability**.

Measuring Volumes Using Water

Did everyone count the same number of drops to reach the one-inch mark?

Who counted the highest number of drops?

Who counted the lowest number of drops?

Different People	Number Drops to One-Inch Mark
Trial One	
Trial Two	
Trial Three	
Trial Four	
Trial Five	

●●

Optional Activity: "M & M" Statistics

Take a bag of M&M candies--plain or peanut. Sort the M&M's by color and arrange in vertical columns--a new column for each color. Have a friend do the same thing with another bag of M&M's. Are the numbers the same? **Variability** occurs in everything. Variation can make Creation interesting. **Can you make a bar graph using the candies?**

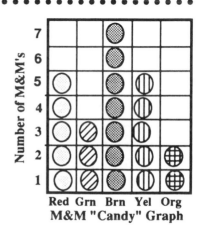

M&M "Candy" Graph

Activity Two - **Measuring How Water Pressure Changes With Depth.**

This simple activity introduces the student to the terms **pressure** and **depth**.   It is also a fun activity that will get the student and surrounding area wet! (In the classrooms, precautions would be prudent.). Using a paper clip, poke two holes by piercing through the middle of a freezer bag. Do the same thing just above the bottom of the bag. Finally, poke the last two holes between the top set and the bottom set.

Fill the freezer bag in a bucket of water. Clasp the top and quickly lift the bag of water out of the bucket. The first time, the student should only observe if there is any difference in how far each water stream "jets" out of the bag.

Refill the bag. Using a ruler the student can try to measure the length of the water stream. The process is repeated until the top, middle, and bottom streams are measured. The measurements are recorded in the student's notebook or on a blackboard.

"Why are the water streams different lengths?"   "What would happen to the water streams if the bag of water is squeezed?" "What would happen to the bottom stream if you had a bigger bag?" "What do you think the term *water pressure* means?"

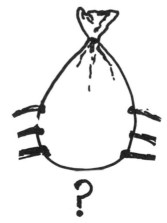

Activity Three - **Air Occupies Space.**

Ideally, this activity is best viewed when using an aquarium. Place a plastic cup in the water. Turn the cup up-side-down with the opening of the cup toward the bottom of the water container. Make sure this cup is full of water. **Ask the student to find a way, using another clear plastic cup, to put air into the cup that is underwater.** As the air replaces the water in the submerged cup, have the student describe what is happening. Even though the student cannot see air, the air is able to force the water from the cup.

How do you fill a cup underwater with air?

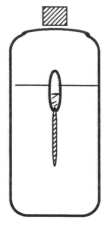

What happens to the eye dropper when you squeeze the sides of the 2-liter bottle?

Activity Three   **Activity Four**

Activity Four - **Air Has The Property Of Pressure.**

The student partially fills an eye dropper with water. Drop the eye dropper into a 2-liter plastic container about three-fourths filled with water. Tighten the lid onto the 2-liter container. **"What happens to the eye dropper?" "What happens to the eye dropper when you squeeze the sides of the plastic container?"**

Did you know that there is almost 400 miles of air on top of you? The air above you is causing a pressure of 15 pounds onto every square inch of your body! Air pressure changes in the atmosphere. Weather reports talk about "low pressure" and "high pressure" systems. Scientists measure changes in air pressure using a tool called a **barometer**. **"Without pressing the sides of the bottle does the eye dropper always float at the same level?"**

Activity Five - Identifying Clouds

Below is a Cloud Identification Chart. The student watches the sky over a predetermined number of days (for example, five days) and records the different cloud types observed. The record is kept by placing a "tally" mark on the line below each cloud type on the chart.

Cloud Identification Chart

Each day you look at the sky record the different cloud types that you see. The record is kept by placing a "tally" mark (⎯Ⅰ⎯) on the line below the cloud type seen. Keep the record for five days. **What type of cloud did you see most often? What type of cloud did you see least frequently?**

INVESTIGATOR LEVEL

Activity Six - **Mixing Substances With Water Forms Solutions.**

Using a rain gauge, the student measures one-inch of water and pours the water into another container. Paper towel dry the cylinder. **"If you add the one-inch of water back into the rain gauge containing the one-inch of salt, will the total volume be two-inches?"**

Once the student makes a prediction, he or she adds the water back into the rain gauge containing the salt. **"What happens?"**

Pour the salt water solution into a plastic cup. Into another plastic cup pour the same volume of pure water. Place both cups in a freezer. Every fifteen minutes the student checks the cups. **"Which cup freezes first?"** **"How does the addition of salt change the *freezing point* of water?"**

Activity Seven - **How Fast Do Ice Cubes Melt?**

"Will six ice cubes melt just as fast as one ice cube?" The student places one ice cube in an aluminum pie pan, two ice cubes in a second pan, three ice cubes in a third, and so on until there are six ice cubes in the sixth pan. Observe the pans containing ice cups at room temperature. The student records the length of time required for the ice to melt in each pan in the table on page 37.

Below the table on page 37 is graph paper. The horizontal scale (across bottom) of the graph is the number of ice cubes in each pan. The vertical scale (up the left side) of the graph is the time for the cubes to melt measured in minutes. The student can graph the time it takes each of the different pans of ice to melt. (If graphing is a concept new to the student, complete the example on page 38.). **"Can you suggest reasons to explain what happened?"**

How Fast Do Ice Cubes Melt?

Time that it takes:

One ice cube to melt	Two ice cubes to melt	Three ice cubes to melt	Four ice cubes to melt	Five ice cubes to melt	Six ice cubes to melt

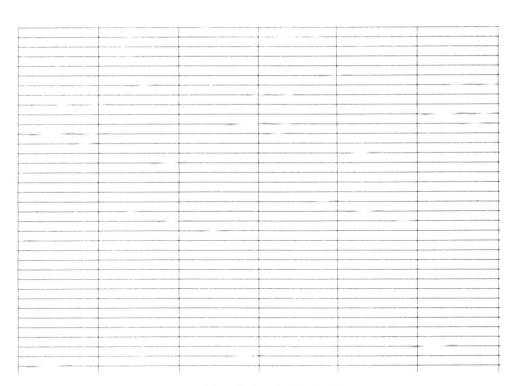

Minutes for All Ice Cubes in Each Pan to Melt

Number of Ice Cubes in Each Pan

What happens when the number of ice cubes in the pan are increased? Give some reasons (hypotheses) why.

Learning How To Graph Data

The table below contains **data** on how long it takes different numbers of ice cubes to melt. Below the table is a graph of some of this data. Can you complete the graph?

Time that it takes:

One ice cube to melt	Two ice cubes to melt	Three ice cubes to melt	Four ice cubes to melt	Five ice cubes to melt	Six ice cubes to melt
65	70	80	95	115	140

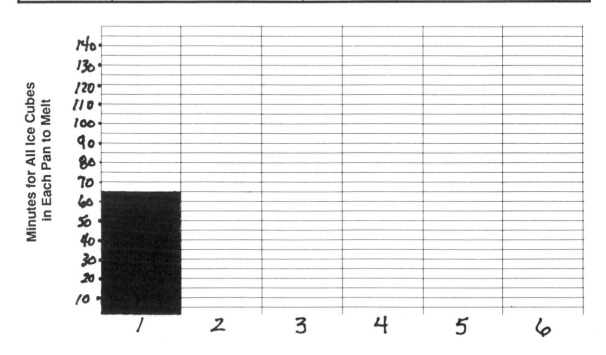

Number of Ice Cubes in
Each Pan

Activity Eight - Air Pressure And Properties Of A Vacuum

Activity Three showed that air pressure can push water out of a container. **"Can the absence of air keep water in a container?"**

Take a clear, plastic 2-liter soft drink bottle and punch a hole the size of a pencil near the bottom. Plug the hole. Fill the bottle about three-fourths full with water and replace the bottle's lid tightly.

The student can mark the outside of the bottle to indicate the water line. **"What will happen when the stopper is removed?" "Will all the water run out of the bottle?"**

After making predictions, remove the stopper. The student will mark the water level when the water quits flowing from the closed bottle. As an additional measuring activity, the amount of time that the water flows from the bottle can be measured with a watch having a second hand.

"Why did the water stop flowing?"

"What would happen if the stoppered bottle was filled to only half full before the stopper was removed?"

Air pressure, or pressure from the atmosphere, cannot enter the closed bottle. As the water escapes through the hole, the air in the bottle cannot take the place of the lost water and a vacuum begins to form. The vacuum that is made because of the absence of air, provides "pull" or **vacuum pressure** to keep the water inside the bottle. **"God created the firmament or atmosphere. Above the firmament is space. Since space is beyond the atmosphere, does a vacuum exist in outer space? Is there air pressure in outer space?"**

Activity Nine - Air and the Property of Kinetic Energy.

Energy is the power to do work--to change something. **Kinetic energy** is the power of motion. Air in motion has kinetic energy, the power to do work. **"What are examples of air powered work?'** (Windmills do a variety of jobs).

In this activity the student constructs a **pinwheel-pulley-color wheel system**. The pinwheel is cut from an eight-inch square of poster board.

Cut the poster board as shown on the dotted line. Fold the outer right angled edges into the center circle and glue--drive a thumb tack into a board to hold the corners in the circle while drying.

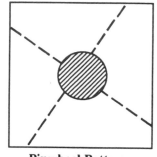

Pinwheel Pattern

Make two pulley cogs. Glue a plastic one-gallon milk carton lid to a cardboard disk. (The inside seal edge of the lid must be removed before glueing.).

Glue the back of the pinwheel onto one of the cogs. Make a hole in the center of the pinwheel and cog. Make sure the cog is next to the one-half inch diameter dowel stick. Put a small nail through the hole and hammer the nail into one end of the dowel. (Length of the dowel is about 14 inches). The pinwheel should spin freely in a breeze.

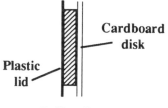

Pulley Cog

Cut a 8-inch diameter disk out of the poster board. Make four equal sections. Color two sections yellow and two sections blue. Glue the side not colored onto the other cog. After drying, make a hole through the disk and cog. Use a small nail attach to the color wheel to the opposite end of the dowel, but on the same side of the dowel as the pinwheel.

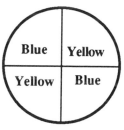

Color Wheel

Tie a piece of twine around both cogs to make a pulley belt. If tied tightly, the pinwheel will not move. If tied loosely, the color wheel will not move. Try tying the twine pulley belt using both patterns shown below. **"What happens when the air moves the pinwheel?" What is different when the pulley pattern changes?"**

Pulley Pattern "A"    **Pulley Pattern "B"**

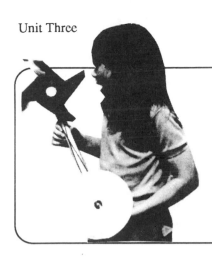

Investigator Level Project

How does the "Pinwheel-Pulley-Color Wheel" System show that air can have the property of **kinetic energy**?

How could the "Pinwheel-Pulley-Color Wheel" System be used to **measure relative air speed**?

Activity Ten - Gases in Air.

The atmosphere or air is made of many different gasses. In this activity the student will experiment with one of those gases. The main gases in air at the earth's surface--at the bottom of the ocean of air-- are nitrogen (78%), oxygen (21%), argon (9%), and carbon dioxide (0.3%). Other gases that exist in smaller amounts at the earth's surface are neon, helium, krypton, hydrogen, and xenon.

Dry ice can be obtained from a variety of sources (check the phone book Yellow Pages). **CAUTION: Dry ice is much colder than water ice. Use heavy gloves when handling dry ice and wear protective goggles or glasses when chipping dry ice.** Have the student research the temperature of dry ice.

Place fragments of dry ice in a large plastic cup. Make a trough out of cardboard. Tilt the trough toward a candle flame at the bottom of the trough. Pour the gas off the cup containing the dry ice and let the gas flow down the trough onto the candle flame.

"What happens to the candle flame?" "What is the gas flowing from the plastic cup containing the crushed dry ice?" "Is this gas heavier than most of the other gases in air?" "Does dry ice go from the state solid to liquid to gas like water ice?"

Burning fossil fuels (gas, oil, and coal) and garbage produces carbon dioxide. **"Will carbon dioxide be mainly found near the earth's surface or high in the atmosphere?"**

How's the Weather?

Optional Weather Activity for Investigator Level
(This page can be photocopied to allow
"weather watching" over a number of days.)

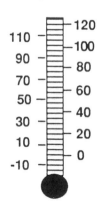

(Draw symbol
on Weather Map
where needed.)

Sunny

Cloudy

Rain

Snow

What is the Temperature Today? Date:_____

(Color in the thermometer for each city's high
temperature for today in degrees Fahrenheit)

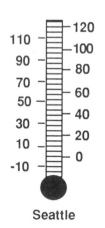

Seattle

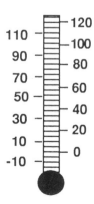

Los Angeles

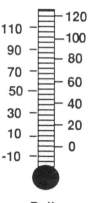

Dallas

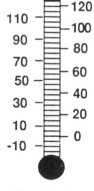

New York

Where You Live

**RESEARCHER
LEVEL**

Activity Eleven - **Properties of the
Atmospheric System--Making Clouds.**
    Models are usually simpler ways to explain
or show how something works. Scientists often
use models of systems in Creation so that they
can better understand how the systems work. In
this activity the student will prepare a model of
cloud formation.

    Cut tho nook of a clear, plastic 2-liter soft drink bottle so that the
opening is about 2 -inches wide.
    CAUTION: Carefully pour <u>hot</u> water into the bottle until the bottle is
approximately one-fifth full. Quickly place over the opening a plastic
sandwich bag containing 4 to 6 ice cubes. Observe what is happening.
"What changes occur in the bottle?" "How does this model relate to
cloud formation in the atmosphere?"

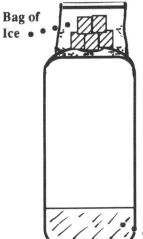

**Bag of
Ice**

• Hot Water

On the basis of this experiment and
your own observations and
experience, develop a diagram and
complete the illustration on page 44
for a Water Cycle Model.

The Water Cycle

Activity Twelve - Humidity: A Property of the Atmosphere.

Humidity is the amount of water vapor in the air. Dry climates, such as deserts have very low humidity. Places near the ocean or in warmer parts near the equator often have high humidity. If fact, the amount of water that the air can hold is affected by temperature. Air at higher temperatures can hold larger amounts of water vapor than air at colder temperatures. The amount of water that air holds at any specific temperature is called **relative humidity**.

Scientists can measure the humidity using a wet and dry bulb thermometer. The student cuts an old shoe lace to a six inch length. One end of the hollow shoe lace is slipped onto the bottom of a thermometer. The other end is threaded into a small hole in the side of a milk or juice carton. The hole is about one inch from the bottom of the carton. Attach the thermometer with the shoe lace to the side of the carton with a rubber band. Position a second thermometer without a shoe lace on the adjoining side of the carton. Finally add water to the container up to the level of the hole.

To find the relative humidity, the student fans the air around the wet bulb thermometer for three to five minutes. This is the wet bulb termperature. After reading the thermometer and recording the temperature in a notebook, the student reads the dry bulb thermometer's temperature.

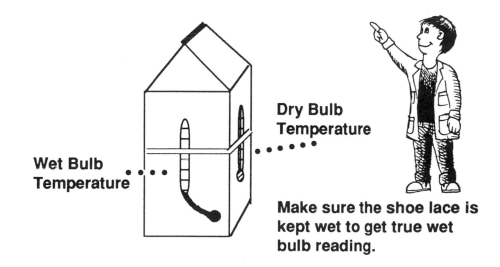

Dry Bulb Temperature

Wet Bulb Temperature

Make sure the shoe lace is kept wet to get true wet bulb reading.

The student substracts the wet bulb temperature from the dry bulb temperature. The difference between wet bulb and dry bulb temperatures is compared to the dry bulb temperature on the table below. For example, if the difference between the wet and dry bulb temperatures is 5 degrees Fahrenheit and the dry bulb temperature is closest to 80 degrees, the table shows that the percent relative humidity is 79%.

Percent Relative Humidity
(using Fahrenheit temperatures)

Difference of Dry Bulb Minus Wet Bulb Temperature

DRY BULB Temperature	1	2	3	4	5	6	7	8	9	10	11	12	13	14	15	16	17	18	19	20	25	30
0	67	33																				
5	73	46	20																			
10	78	56	34	13																		
15	82	64	46	29	11																	
20	85	70	55	40	26	12																
25	87	74	62	49	37	25	13															
30	89	78	67	56	46	36	26	16														
35	91	81	72	63	54	45	36	27	19	10												
40	92	83	75	68	60	52	45	37	29	22	15											
45	93	86	78	71	64	57	51	44	38	31	25	18	12									
50	93	87	80	74	67	61	55	49	43	38	32	27	21	16	10							
55	94	88	82	76	70	65	59	54	49	43	38	33	28	23	19	14						
60	94	89	83	78	73	68	63	58	53	48	43	39	34	30	26	21	17	13				
65	95	90	85	80	75	70	66	61	56	52	48	44	39	35	31	27	24	20	16	12		
70	95	90	86	81	77	72	68	64	59	55	51	48	44	40	36	33	29	25	22	19		
75	96	91	86	82	78	74	70	66	62	58	54	51	47	44	40	37	34	30	27	24		
80	96	91	87	83	79	75	72	68	64	61	57	54	50	47	44	41	38	35	32	29	15	
85	96	92	88	84	80	76	73	69	66	62	59	56	52	49	46	43	41	38	35	32	20	
90	96	92	89	85	81	78	74	71	68	65	61	58	55	52	49	47	44	41	39	36	24	
95	96	93	89	85	82	79	75	72	69	66	63	60	57	54	51	49	46	43	41	38	27	
100	96	93	89	86	83	80	77	73	70	68	65	62	59	56	54	51	49	46	44	41	30	21
	97	93	90	87	83	80	77	74	71	69	66	63	60	58	55	53	50	48	46	43	33	23

Activity Thirteen - Air, Water, Vibration, and Sound.

In Unit Two, the student learned about the Wave Theory of Light--light of different colors occurs in different wavelengths. Light is part of the **electromagnetic spectrum of energy**. The many wavelengths of the electromagnetic spectrum go from very short to very long. Here is a partial list of of wavelengths belonging to this spectrum: cosmic rays, X-rays, light rays, radio waves, TV, microwaves, and sound waves.

Take a piece of board (approximately 4" x 9" x 1") and hammer two nails, one each into opposite ends of the board. Tie a length of twine to the two opposing nails. Repeat the procedure with two more nails and a piece of fishing line or thin wire between these two nails. A stretched, vibrating string is the basis for musical instruments such as a violin, guitar, and piano. The tone produced from the string depends on the string length, mass, and how tight the string is "strung." High tones produce shorter sound wavelengths--lower tones form longer sound wavelengths.

Pluck the twine as you would a guitar. Time the duration of the sound with the second hand on a watch. Repeat with the fishing line or thin wire string. Have the student describe the difference in sound. Repeat with both strings for two more trials, recording results on the table below.

Place the sound board in a fish tank three-fourths filled with water, or in about six to eight inches of water in a sink, or if at home, in a bathtub. Pluck the twine and fishing line strings. Again, record the duration of the sound.

"How is the sound different between the two strings in air?" "Which string has the longest wavelength?" "How did the sound made by the strings change underwater?" "Was the sound wavelengths of the two strings made longer or shorter by being underwater?"

**Twine and Fishing
Line Sound Board**

Trial	Sound in Air Time (seconds)	Sound in Water Time (seconds)
#1		
#2		
#3		

Activity Fourteen - **Newton's Third Law Races.**

Isaac Newton developed three laws of motion. **Newton's third law simply stated is that for every action there is an equal and opposite reaction.** This is easily demonstrated with an inflated balloon. While the end of the balloon is held closed, the air pressure inside is pushing equally in all directions. But when the student lets go of the balloon, the air rushes out and the balloon flies around the room--the air is escaping in one direction and the balloon is travelling in the opposite direction.

This activity is suited for groups of students working as teams to produce the fastest JPV (jet propulsion vehicle), but can also easily be done by students at home. The student tapes a straw to an inflated balloon. A guide string (for example, dental floss) is threaded throught the straw taped to the balloon. For Newton's Third Law Race, each team has its own JPV and guideline. Often after demonstrating the principle, I will let teams design and test their own systems.

The teams let their balloons go at the same time, with the winning JPV crossing the finish-line first. The distance from starting- line to finish-line should be about 20 feet.

Activity Fifteen - Testing for Gases in the Atmosphere.

Oxygen gas is part of the atmosphere and extremely important to living organisms. Oxygen also makes its presence known by reaction with other elements such as iron (symbol Fe)--it combines with **(oxidizes)** iron causing rust or iron oxide. This property of oxygen can be made the basis of a test for oxygen gas in the atmosphere.

Wash steel wool with soapy water to remove any oils. Place about one-inch of steel wool in the bottom of a test tube (any tube will do, including a rain gauge). Position a bent paper clip on top of the steel wool to keep the wool from falling out when the tube is inverted.

Fill a baby food jar half-full of water. Place the tube containing the steel wool open end down into the water. Using a ruler, measure the height of air in the tube and record this measurement on the table below. Repeat this measuring procedure over several days. **"What is happening to the steel wool?" "What changes are occurring in the volume of air in the tube?"** Have the student develop a hypothesis of what is taking place.

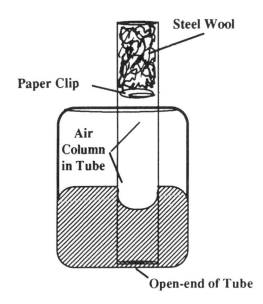

Date	Height of Air in Tube

Activity Sixteen - **Testing Water Quality**.

Water is important to all life. Even though the majority of the earth's surface is water, only a small amount is available for humans, animals and plants. The oceans represent about 70% of the earth's surface, but their waters are too salty to sustain the life of most land plants and animals. One reason the oceans are salty is because these are the Flood waters mentioned in the Bible. Before the worldwide Flood, the seas possibly were not as salty as they are today.

One test for water quality is hardness. **Water hardness** is related to what minerals and how many are dissolved in the water--the more minerals in the water, the harder the water. Minerals in water combine with soap. This is what causes the "soap ring" in a bathtub. Pure, or distilled, water is free of minerals. Soap in pure water easily forms soap bubbles. The harder the water, the more soap required to make bubbles.

Collect water samples from different sources; for example, tap water, distilled water from the grocery store, rain water, ocean water, pond water, or river water. Select baby food jars of equal size. Fill each half-full with a different water sample adding the same amount of water to each jar.

Use an eye dropper to drop liquid soap into one of the sample jars--one drop at a time. After adding each drop place a lid on the jar and shake for 15 seconds. Continue to add liquid soap one drop at a time until soap bubbles remain for 3 minutes after shaking. If the soap bubbles collapse, add another drop of liquid soap. Have the student make a chart with headings like the one below on which to record results. **"Which sample of water is hardest?"** Have the student *rank* the water samples from softest to hardest.

Water Sample	Number of Soap Drops	Hardness Rank

Measuring Volumes Using Water

Did everyone count the same number of drops to reach the one-inch mark?

Who counted the highest number of drops?

Who counted the lowest number of drops?

Different People	Number Drops to One-inch Mark
Trial One	
Trial Two	
Trial Three	
Trial Four	
Trial Five	

Researcher Level Activity

Scientists often use a group of math tools called **statistics**. The statistical **average** is one of those tools. For example, if you are average height for your age, then half of all people your age will be your height or taller and the other half will be your height or smaller.

"What are the average number of drops in the measuring experiment above?"

You can answer this question by adding all five "trials" together and then dividing by 5 (the number of trials). This gives you the average number of drops in one-inch!

Who Am I?

(Below are clues from the life of a famous scientist who worked with oceans and the atmosphere. The scientist's identity is given on bottom of the References, page 132.)

Most of my work was done with the United States Navy. One time when I was ill in bed, my son was reading to me from the Bible. This day he was reading from the book of Psalms, chapter 8. What particularly caught my attention was verse 8 where the Bible talked about "paths in the seas." Since God created everything and since He also inspired the men who wrote the Bible, I realized that we should be able to find these "paths in the seas."

I began by giving captains of sailing ships instructions to write their position at sea on a piece of paper. The paper was to be sealed in a bottle and thrown overboard. The paper also had instructions for the person who found the bottle. He was to write down where the bottle was found and send the paper back to me.

On the basis of these experiments, I was able to plot the currents and winds of the Atlantic Ocean. For this reason I was known as "The Pathfinder of the Seas" and considered by many to be the founder of the modern science of oceanography--the study of the oceans.

All this happened becaused I believed God when He inspired the psalmist to write about the paths of the seas. On my tombstone at the U.S. Naval Academy is written--as you can probably already guess--the eighth Psalm. Who am I?

(Reference: *Men of Science/Men of God* by H. Morris. 1988.)

Land and Plants
Day Three of Creation

"Let the waters below the heavens be gathered into one place, and let dry land appear"..."Let the earth sprout vegetation, plants yielding seed, and fruit trees bearing fruit after their kind, with seed in them, on the earth."..And there was evening and there was morning, the third day. **Genesis 1: 9 -13.**

God Created Land and the Plants
Learning Objectives

Explorer Level. The student will: -
* Investigate minerals in Scripture;
* Describe where rocks are found and how they are used;
* Investigate how soil can be made from rocks;
* Observe the process of germination;
* Observe and draw conclusions on how plants interact with water;
* Identify and describe the parts of a plant.

Investigator Level. The student will: -

* Evaluate minerals using the property of hardness
* Investigate and classify using rock properties;
* Compare the germination of monocotyledon and dicotyledon seeds;
* Demonstrate how plants interact with the atmosphere (transpiration);
* Experiment with plants interacting with light.
* Experiment with plants as chemical energy systems.

Researcher Level. The student will: -

* Experiment with mineral crystallization and recognize symmetry in minerals;
* Recognize the relationship between rock type and location in the environment;
* Determine by experiment the relationship of energy to seed germination;
* Determine by experiment and research the relationship of pigmentation and light utilization by plants;
* Experiment with and develop a concept of acids and bases, and chemical reactions.

Material Preparation

Explorer Level Activities. Bible; access to some examples of minerals; two rocks (preferably different types); variety of seeds; 4 plastic cups; paper towels; celery; red and blue food coloring; shallow pie pan; eye dropper.

Investigator Level Activities. Bible; access to some samples of minerals; penny; piece of glass; 10 -15 each of bean and corn seeds; access to rocks; 2 geranium (or tomato) plants in pots; 3 black plastic squares (1" by 2"); two large freezer bags; lemon, penny, nickel.

Researcher Level Activities. Access to a rocks and minerals handbook; hand magnifier; rock salt, a pint glass jar; twine; test tube or small olive jar; one-hole stopper or soft modeling clay; 2 thermometers (Celsius or Fahrenheit); 30 - 40 pea seeds; absorbent cotton or glass wool; alcohol; paper coffee filter; geranium; graph paper, 4 small flower pots, 12 seeds, coffee can, gallon jug to carry water, watch; vinegar, baking soda, alum, ammonia cleaner; red cabbage, plastic test tube with stopper.

Teacher Guidelines and Activities

**EXPLORER
LEVEL**

Activity One - Minerals in the Bible.

Minerals are different from rocks. Rocks are composed of minerals. This activity introduces the student to some mineral names that are found in the Bible. Read Exodus 28: 16 - 20 to the student.

The chart on page 54 represents the breastplate worn by the High Priest in ancient Israel. The student can (a) look up each mineral name in a mineral handbook or other suitable reference then draw and color the appropriate square on the Ephod (*ee' fod*) illustration; or (b) collect and glue minerals onto the illustration.

"What are some properties of minerals?" Have the student collect pieces of rocks common to your area. Mix rock and mineral specimens together. Ask the student to choose which are minerals. **"What properties make rocks different from minerals?"**

Activity Two - Rocks: God's Building Blocks

There are three types of rocks: sedimentary, igneous, and metamorphic. **Sedimentary rocks** (sandstones and limestones) for the most part are the result of the worldwide Flood described in Genesis. **Igneous rocks** come from beneath the Earth's surface and are the foundation rocks for the ocean basins (basalts) or for the continents (granites). **Metamorphic rocks** (shists and shales) are igneous and sedimentary rocks that have been heated and squeezed under tremendous pressures. If possible, show the student samples of each type of rock.

Have the student survey his or her home and neighborhood. **"How are rocks used?"** Make a bulletin board or poster display of pictures for different uses of rocks.

Activity Three - Making Soil From Rocks

Have the student select two rocks (preferrably different kinds of rocks)--both about fist size. Rub the rocks together over a white piece of paper. Have the student describe what happens.

Then have the student bring soil from a flower bed or garden. Compare the soil made by rubbing the rocks together with the soil from outside. Have the student use a hand magnifier, if available. **"What properties are the same between the two samples?" "What properties are different?"**

As an optional project have the student plant 2 - 3 seeds in a paper cup containing flower bed soil and do the same for the soil made from rubbing the two rocks together. Label each cup. Over time the student can observe and report on the experiment.

Activity Four - God Made Plants To Reproduce After Their Own Kind.

Dicotyledon seeds have two observable halves--for example bean and pea seeds. **Monocotyledon seeds** do not--the seed appears to be whole as with corn, grasses and most grains. Give the student 6 to 8 seeds (if possible a mixture of monocotyledon and dicotyledon).

The student prepares a **seed germination** "chamber" as shown below. The seeds are placed about half-way down between the clear plastic cup's side and the paper towel.

The student should examine and draw the seed embryos as they germinate and begin to grow. **"What properties are different between the dicotyledon and monocotyledon seeds?"**

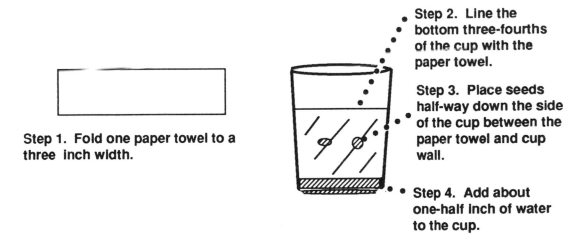

Step 1. Fold one paper towel to a three inch width.

Step 2. Line the bottom three-fourths of the cup with the paper towel.

Step 3. Place seeds half-way down the side of the cup between the paper towel and cup wall.

Step 4. Add about one-half inch of water to the cup.

When the **seedlings** have grown even with the cup's rim, pour off the water and turn the cup upside down--resting the cup rim on two parallel pencils. Periodically moisten the paper in the cup. **"Do the seedlings continue to grow upside down?"** **"What direction do the roots begin to grow?"** **"What can this tell us about God's design in plants?"**

On page 58, the student can label the major parts (leaf, stem, roots) of a plant, and the major parts (cotyledon, seed husk, root) of a germinating seed.

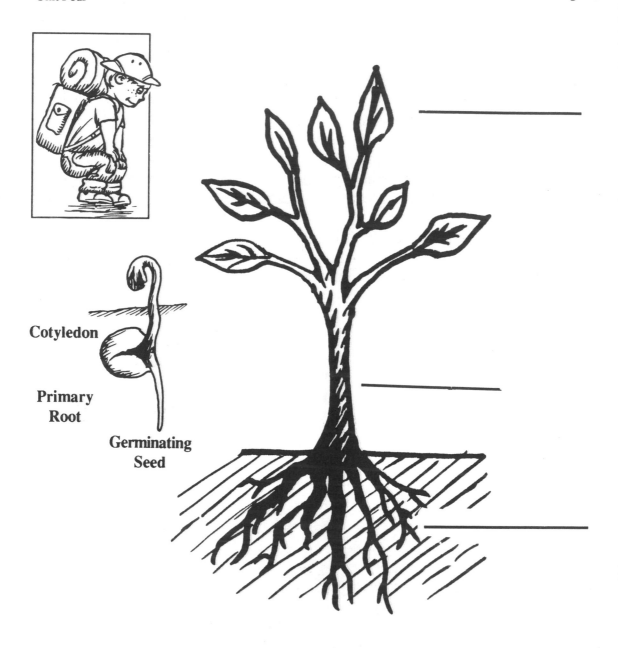

Cotyledon

Primary
Root

Germinating
Seed

Name the Parts of the Plant

Activity Five - **God Made Plants To Interact With Soil.**
   "What do plants get from the soil?" To answer this question the student will conduct an experiment using celery (very leafy).
   Hold the base of the fresh celery stalk underwater. With a razor blade make a fresh cut straight across the base of the stalk. Next split the stalk up from the base about 4 inches. Gently bend each half into separate, side-by-side, clear plastic cups of water. With an eye dropper add five drops of red food coloring to one cup and five drops of blue food coloring to the other cup. Place the cups and stalks on the window sill.

The student records observations in his notebook with colored drawings.

**Plastic Cups Containing Water
and Different Food Coloring**

   One important way that soil and plants interact is that plant roots going throughout the soil provides support-- soil and roots interact to keep the plant from falling over.   Through its roots a plant gets water and **nutrients** that are held in the soil. The plant stalk has **capillary tubes** that draw the water up all the way to the leaves. Using energy from sunlight, the water and nutrients are **transformed** into new plant **cells and tissues**. Special tissues that transport water from the roots to the leaves are called **xylem** (*zye lem'*).

The Ephod, worn by the High Priest of ancient Israel, had a breastplate that contained four rows of minerals. Each mineral represented one of the twelve tribes of Israel. (Exodus 28: 16 - 20).

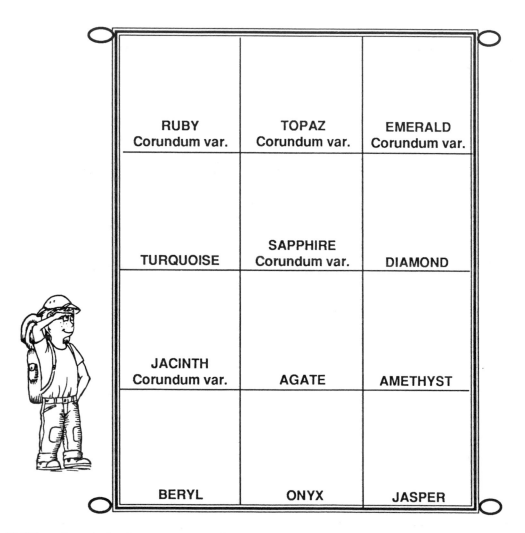

RUBY Corundum var.	**TOPAZ** Corundum var.	**EMERALD** Corundum var.
TURQUOISE	**SAPPHIRE** Corundum var.	**DIAMOND**
JACINTH Corundum var.	**AGATE**	**AMETHYST**
BERYL	**ONYX**	**JASPER**

Will minerals be part of Christ's New Creation?
(Read Revelation 21: 19 -20 to the student.)

**INVESTIGATOR
LEVEL**

Activity Seven - **Minerals and the Property of Hardness.**

Minerals have several properties that are useful in their classification. One such property is hardness. A hardness scale has been created and is called **Moh's Hardness Scale** (not named, incidentally, after one of the Three Stooges).

The scale goes from a value of one for the softest minerals to ten for the hardest mineral, which is diamond.

In this activity the student will experiment and classify minerals according to hardness, using common materials of known hardness as described on page 67.

Activity Eight - **Rocks: Properties and Environments.**

The chart on page 62 shows different environments in which rocks are found. This chart can be copied. Have the student color each environment a different color and collect as many rocks as possible and glue them on the chart. This is a good opportunity to use a rock and mineral handbook to identify the listed rock types.

ROCKS: GOD'S BUILDING BLOCKS

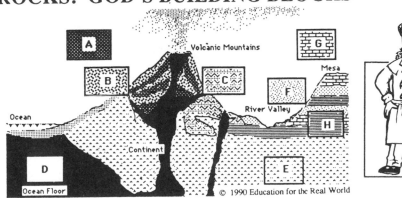

© 1990 Education for the Real World

ROCKS: GOD'S BUILDING BLOCKS

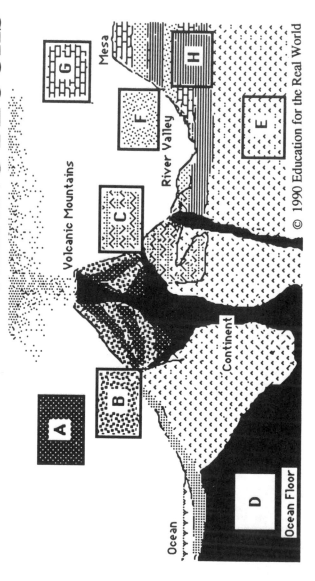

© 1990 Education for the Real World

A - Lavas are basalts ejected from volcanos. Typically they have holes like Swiss cheese caused by gas bubbles formed as the lava hardened. B - Tuff is a sedimentary rock formed when volcanic ash is cemented into rock. C - Schist is a metamorphic rock made from the minerals mica and quartz. D - Basalt are igneous rocks and are the foundation rocks of the ocean basins. E - Granites are also igneous rocks, and are the foundation rocks of the continents. F - Sandstones are sedimentary rocks formed when sand is cemented together. G - Limestones are sedimentary rocks often made from the calcium shells of billions of marine creatures. Both sandstones and limestones are evidence of the worldwide destruction caused during the Biblical Flood. H - Shales are formed from fine clays and many times the decompsed remains of organisms.

Rock Genesis and Classification

Activity Nine - Plants Interact with the Atmosphere

Plants take **carbon dioxide** gases from the atmosphere and release back **oxygen** during the process of respiration. Plants also release water into the air in a process called **transpiration**. By analogy, humans release water containing waste products through the pores in our skin. This process called "sweating" is also transpiration. Plants release water into the atmosphere through pores on their leaves called **stomata**.

"What forms on the inside of the bag around the plant?"

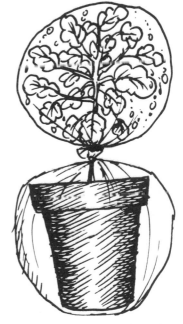

The student wraps a flower pot containing a tomato or geranium in a plastic bag. Make sure the bag hasn't any holes. Gather the bag over the top of the pot and around the base of the plant where the stem meets the soil. Use a twist tie to seal the bag. Next, place a larger plastic bag (without holes) over the top of the plant down to where the stem meets the soil. As before, seal the bag.

Place the plant on a table or shelf, but <u>not</u> in direct sunlight (temperatures inside the bag will be too hot). Observe the plant on the following day. **"What has collected on the inside of the bag that is over the plant?" "How does this experiment show that plants give up moisture to the atmosphere?"**

Activity Ten - **How Plants Interact with Light.**

     The student needs three flower pots containing three 2" tall seedlings (any plant will do). The flower pots should be the same size-- 4 - 6 inches diameter across the top of the pot. The student collects two plastic 2-liter soft drink bottles. One bottle is clear plastic and the other is green. Cut the top portions off of each bottle.

     Make three flaps around the cut edges of each bottle. Next make three flaps around the "domed" part of the bottle.

     Invert the domes over the seedlings in the flower pots. Place the seedlings on the window sill, but <u>not</u> in direct sunlight. Twice weekly the student removes both domes, observes the seedlings and measures each seedling's growth.   Allow this activity to continue for three weeks.

     "What properties are different between plants the green plastic dome and the clear dome?" "Are the plants the same color?" "Why were flaps cut into the domes?" "What would happened to the plants if the flaps were closed and sealed with tape?" "Can you give some reasons (hypotheses) to explain what was observed?"

Activity Eleven - **Plants and Electrical Energy.**

The student has worked with a battery to produce a closed system allowing an electrical current to light a bulb (Activity Nine, page 21). Now the student can observe the chemicals inside a plant fruit--a lemon--interact with elements in two metals to produce an weak electrical charge.

The student or teacher cuts two parallel slits into a lemon. The slits should be close together--about the width of a nickel apart. Next the student places a copper penny (a penny with a date before 1980) into one slit and a nickel into the other slit. Arrange the two coins so that the portions in the lemon are almost touching.

Have the student touch his or her tongue to the exposed portions of both coins at the same time. (The coins can be cleaned by placing them in lemon juice. The effect of the lemon juice on the coins can also be observed by the student). When the student's tongue touches, he should feel a mild electrical shock or tingling. The plant fruit has become a battery--even if it is a weak one!

Nickel

Penny

Lemon

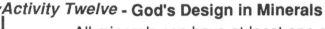

**RESEARCHER
LEVEL**

Activity Twelve - **God's Design in Minerals**

All minerals can have at least one of the six, three-dimensional, crystal systems. These six systems are shown on page 67. Optional activity: The teacher may have the student construct three-dimensional copies of these geometric systems. The student may also want to find the common minerals given as examples on the chart, and glue each mineral onto a copy of the chart.

CAUTION: Since this activity requires working with hot water, adult supervision is required.

In creation crystals of salt occur naturally from a chemical process similar to that used in this activity. As a **saturated** salt or brine solution **evaporates**, mineral crystals form. These halite (*hay' lite*) crystals have the properties of an *isometric* **crystal system** (a cubic symmetry and design). The size of the crystal formed depends partially on how quickly or slowly the crystallization process goes.

The student fills a pyrex measuring cup (two cup capacity) with rock salt or table salt up to the one cup mark. Next the teacher, or student with supervision, adds near boiling water to the same one cup mark. Stir the salt and water mixture with a plastic spoon for about three minutes. Pour only the liquid into another glass container. Place one end of a piece of twine into the liquid with the other end of the twine outside the container. Allow to cool, undisturbed. Observe the container from time to time throughout the day. **"Do you know how long it took for crystals to begin forming?" "Where did the crystals begin forming first?"**

After one day remove the twine and examine the crystals under a magnifier. The student will describe the shape of crystals seen.

Repeat the experiment, but this time allow the crystal to cool in a refrigerator. **"What properties are different between the two crystals formed at the two different temperatures?" "What explanation (hypothesis) can you make to account for the observed differences?"**

Hardness Property of Minerals

Hardness. All minerals are not the same hardness. Hardness is tested by scratching the mineral's surface. A measure of hardness is called the Mohs' Hardenss Scale. The scale is represented by ten common minerals, arranged in order of increasing hardness:

Hardness	Mineral	Hardness	Mineral
1	Talc	6	Orthoclase
2	Gypsum	7	Quartz
3	Calcite	8	Topaz
4	Fluorite	9	Corundum
5	Apatite	10	Diamond

Other common items that are of known hardness can be used to test the hardness property of minerals. A fingernail is 2.5, a copper penny is 3, and glass is 5.5. Scratch a mineral across these surfaces. If the mineral scratches the surface, the mineral has a hardness more than that of the scratched surface.

Crystal System Property of Minerals

Cubic		Orthorhombic	
	Ex: Halite		Ex: Topaz
Hexagonal		Monoclinic	
	Ex: Quartz		Ex: Gypsum
Tetragonal		Triclinic	
	Ex: Chalcopyrite		Ex: Rhodonite

Activity Thirteen - Acids and Bases.

Elements can form chemical compounds and some compounds exist in the form of crystals. Alum is a chemical compound that can also exist as a crystal. Alum, like sodium chloride, is a salt. When some salts, like alum, are dissolved in water, they form **acids**. Other salts, like lye (sodium hydroxide), form **bases** when dissolved.

In this activity the student will be introduced to the concept of acids and bases as a way of classifying solutions made from salts.

The student (and teacher) will prepare an **acid-base indicator** from the leaves of red cabbage. Select several leaves with a deep purple pigment and place is a small amount of water in the bottom of a pan (approximately one-fifth cup). Boil the water until it has turned purple. Allow the water to cool before pouring into several clear, small plastic cups. The more purple color in the water, the better the results. Each cup should contain at least one-half inch of purple liquid.

Have the student dissolve one tablespoon of alum (available in grocery stores) in one-fourth cup of water. Stir the alum to dissolve and pour into an empty plastic cup. Repeat the same procedure using baking soda in place of alum.

Using an eye dropper, the student, drop-by-drop, adds the alum solution to one of the plastic cups containing the purple leaf extract. **"What happens to the color of the purple acid-base indicator in the plastic cup?"** Continue to add alum solution until a color change is permanent. Repeat the procedure using the baking soda solution. **"Is the color change the same or different?"**

Repeat the procedure a third and fourth time using vinegar and liquid ammonia cleaner. Have the student list the names of the solutions and what effect the solutions had on the purple acid-base indicator. (Acids turn the purple indicator red; bases turn the indicator a greenish color.). Have the student classify each solution as either acid or base.

Have the student soak a coffee filter in any remaining purple acid-base indicator extract. Allow the filter to air dry. After drying the filter may be cut into thin strips. The student now has an acid-base indicator paper, also known as *litmus paper*.

Activity Fourteen - Chemical Cannons.

Using the chemical solutions from Activity Thirteen, page 68, the student will study the ability of chemicals to react.

Place the four solutions (alum, vinegar, ammonia, and sodium bicarbonate) in labelled plastic cups. Allow the student to choose any two solutions.

The student adds one of the two solutions to a plastic test tube (or any plastic tube, such as a rain gauge). The student adds the second solution and quickly stoppers the tube (wax coated cork, plastic, or rubber stoppers are preferred).

CAUTION: Plastic tubes are much safer than glass. If buying test tubes, remember that most serious cuts occur from glass breaks around the tops of tubes. As a service, the author will supply two **FREE** plastic test tubes with stoppers. Send a self-addressed envelope with sufficient return postage for 2 ounces to: David Unfred, 3601 42nd Street, Lubbock, TX 79413.

Holding the tube (chemical cannon) away from the student, the cannon will shoot the stopper, if the right two chemicals were chosen. If the first choice produced a dud, have the student reconsider the problem and choose again.

Vinegar or alum (both acids) when mixed with sodium bicarbonate (a base) will react to release carbon dioxide gas. The pressure from the gas will propel the stopper.

Students can have a chemical cannon races measuring the distance each student's stopper travels. Should we also add that this activity be done outside?

Activity Fifteen - Seeds and Energy.

Plant seeds produce heat energy during the germination process. This heat results when the embryonic plant **oxidizes** the food stored in the seed. The student will measure the heat produced from the germination process.

The student places absorbent cotton in the bottom of a thermos. The cotton should reach to within three inches of the top of the thermos. Add water to the top level of the cotton in the thermos.

Fill the remaining space in the thermos with blackeyed pea or bean seeds. Put a thermometer bulb down into the middle of the seeds. Make sure that enough of the thermometer extends above the thermos so that you can read the thermometer. Seal the top of the thermos with modeling clay (a non-hardening variety).

Once the thermos is sealed, the student records the temperature on page 71. Observe the termperature twice daily over the next four days. Record temperature observations on page 71. At the end of the experiment, the student can plot the temperature data on the graph provided. (Connect the plotted data with a line.) **"What hypothesis might explain why heat is produced by the seeds?" "In what ways are the seeds different after the experiment from before the experiment?"**

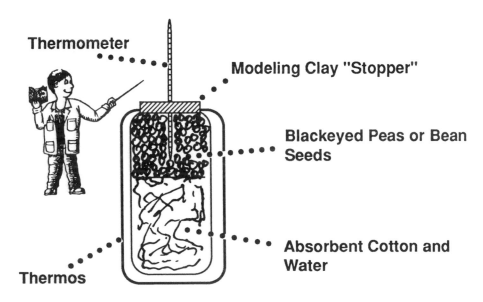

Thermometer

Modeling Clay "Stopper"

Blackeyed Peas or Bean Seeds

Absorbent Cotton and Water

Thermos

Time

Temperature

Temperature: ____ ____   ____ ____   ____ ____   ____ ____

Time: ____ ____   ____ ____   ____ ____   ____ ____

Day: _____   _____   _____   _____

Activity Sixteen - Separating Plant Leaf Pigments

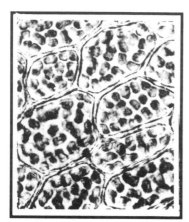

Chloroplasts in the plant cell are the uniquely created "factories" where plant pigments such as chlorophyll transform light energy into biochemical energy.

Paper chromotography is a tool scientists use to identify unknown substances. A substance is transferred onto an absorbent paper--for example, a paper towel or coffee filter. As a **solvent** moves up the paper, the substance travels with the solvent. Substances can be identified by how far up the paper they move. Since different substances move at different rates, a mixture of substances can be **separated** and the different substances **identified.**

The student cuts a strip from a coffee filter or paper towel about one inch wide and four to six inches long. Next remove a dark green leaf from the geranium. Place the leaf at one end of the paper strip. One inch above the end of the paper strip rub the edge of a penny across the leaf leaving a narrow green mark on the paper.

Repeat this procedure several times using different parts of the leaf. Tape the opposite end of the paper strip to a pencil and place into a glass container containing the solvent **rubbing alcohol.** IMPORTANT: The narrow line must be above the level of the solvent in the container.

When the solvent has travelled up the length of the paper strip, remove the paper **chromatogram** from the solvent and let it dry.

"How far did color pigment travel from the original narrow band?" Are there any other color pigments in addition to green on the chromatogram?" "What is the name of the green pigment?" "What are some names of other pigments that are found in leaves?"

Activity Seventeen - Soil Environments.

Soils come in four types: gravel, sand, loam, and clay. In reality, soils may also vary between these four types. A **gravel** is coarse with many pebbles. **Sand** is coarse to fine grains with no (or only isolated) pebbles. **Loam** soils are typically a dark color with soft texture. **Clay** soils are smooth and slimy or sticky when wet.

The student will collect all four types of soils (if available). Collect enough soil to use in small flower pots. Plant 2 or 3 seeds in each soil type. Using a measuring cup, add the same amount of water to the plantings in each soil type. When watering continue to add the <u>same</u> amount of water to each pot. Over time the students can observe and record results. At various times plant growth can be measured using a ruler. After four to six weeks, have the student graph results as a bar graph (example below).

Next, the student will study the property of soil porosity. Porosity in soils are their ability to hold water. In this phase of the activity the student will take a coffee can with both ends removed. Make a mark on the inside of the can about a third of the way up from the "bottom". Porosity will be measured by setting the can, bottom-end, firmly on the ground and pouring water into the can up to the inside mark. The student observes the amount of time that it takes the water to soak into the soil. The porosity can be measured in several different locations--hopefully over a wide area. The student can make a map of the area, placing a dot and the soak time at each soil location studied. **"What soil type has the highest porosity (fastest time to soak-up the water)?" "What soil type has the least porosity (longest time)?"**

EXAMPLE   **Bar Graph of Plant Growth in Different Soil Types**

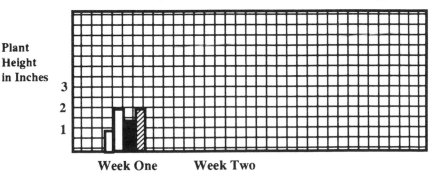

Legend
☐ = Gravel
☐ = Sand
■ = Loam
▨ = Clay

Who Am I?

(Below are clues from the life of a famous scientist. The scientist's identity is given on bottom of the References, page 132.)

Many scholars call me the father of modern chemistry.

As a Christian, I believed in the careful study of God's Word, the Bible. I was interested in missions and contributed much of the money the Lord provided me toward Bible translation work.

I was also very interested in Christian apologetics, that is, the defense of Christianity, and even gave a series of lectures proving the Christian religion.

Throughout my life I made many contributions to the sciences of physics and chemistry. A fundamental law relating gas pressures to temperature and volume bears my name.

Some of my discoveries you may have repeated in this unit. For example, I defined acids as compounds that, in water solutions, taste sour, turn the dye litmus from blue to red, neutralize bases, and react with some metals to give off hydrogen gas.

Finally, I was also one of the founders of one of the most famous associations of scientists in Europe, the Royal Society of London.

Who am I?

(Reference: *Men of Science/Men of God* by H. Morris. 1988.)

UNIT FIVE

Sun, Moon, and Stars
Day Four of Creation

"Let there be lights in the expanse of the heavens to separate the day from the night, and let them be for signs, and for seasons, and for days and years; and let them give light on the earth"... And there was evening and there was morning, the fourth day. Genesis 1: 14, 19.

God Made the Sun, Moon and Stars

Learning Objectives

Explorer Level. The student will: -
* Identify major constellations;
* Gain a Biblical understanding of constellations;
* Record and observe changes in the phases of the Moon;
* Use the Sun to track time and make fractional estimates of time;
* Use a model to understand seasons.

Investigator Level. The student will: -
* Identify major constellations in the night sky;
* Identify individual stars in constellations;
* Construct and use an astrolab to observe and record star movement in the night sky;
* Develop a model to understand how the Earth, Sun and Moon interact to produce the Moon's phases and to produce an eclipse;

Researcher Level. The student will: -
* Construct and use a reflective telescope;
* Understand principles of a reflective telescope;
* Understand the terms apogee and perigee;
* Propose a catastrophe model for the Moon using observations and the Biblical record;
* Observe sunspots;
* Understand that sunspots interact with the atmosphere;
* Design an experiment to evaluate the "greenhouse effect".

Materials and Preparation

Explorer Level Activities. Potato chip can (e.g., Pringles) with one or more plastic lids; straight pin and thin nail; glue; black construction paper; flashlight; 2-inch diameter poster board disk; 16" by 16" white poster board; sissors; an orange and tooth picks; resource materials showing the different seasons.

Investigator Level Activities. Protractor; wooden ruler or similar straight edge; tape; thread; washer; thumb tack.

Researcher Level Activities. Six inch cosmotic concave (image enlarging) mirror; binoculars (inexpensive); large rubber bands; 3 wing nuts and bolts; 1" by 2" by 2 - feet wooden strip; large (12" length by 12" width) cardboard box; white poster board; two thermometers (Fahrenheit or Centigrade); one 2 -liter clear plastic soft drink bottle; one 2 - liter green plastic soft drink bottle; 4 pans or bowls that will fit inside the 2 - liter soft drink bottles.

**EXPLORER
LEVEL**

Activities

Activity One - God Made and Named the Stars.

He counts the number of the stars: He gives names to all of them. Great is our Lord, and abundant in strength; His understanding is infinite.
Psalm 147: 2 - 3.

Then the Lord answered Job out of the whirlwind and said,....."Can you bind the chains of the Pleiades, or loose the cords of Orion? Can you lead forth a constellation in its season, and guide the Bear with her sons? Do you know the ordinances of the heavens, or fix their rule over the earth? "
Job 38: 31 - 33.

From the Creation Week, God has established the stars as signs. It was a star that led the magi to Jesus after His birth. Some Bible teachers have considered the possibility that groups of stars, called **constellations**, were organized together from earliest times to provide mankind with a visual story of the Gospel. Over time, the story told was distorted. Today constellations serve as convenient "roadsigns" that help us explore the heavens.

The student constructs a star scope from a small diameter can, such as the popular potato chip containers. Cut a half inch diameter hole in the bottom end of the container and cut-out the center of the plastic lid, leaving about a quarter inch ring around the hole.

Using the constellation patterns (or a photocopy of the patterns) on page 79, the student glues these onto black construction paper. Next cut-out each disk. The constellation disk is fitted into the plastic lid ring. Use a straight pin to punch-out the small stars and a thin nail to punch-out the larger stars.

When the plastic ring and constellation disk is placed on the container, the star scope is complete. The student looks through the open end and sees the constellation as it appears in the night sky.

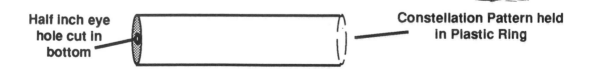

Half inch eye hole cut in bottom

Constellation Pattern held in Plastic Ring

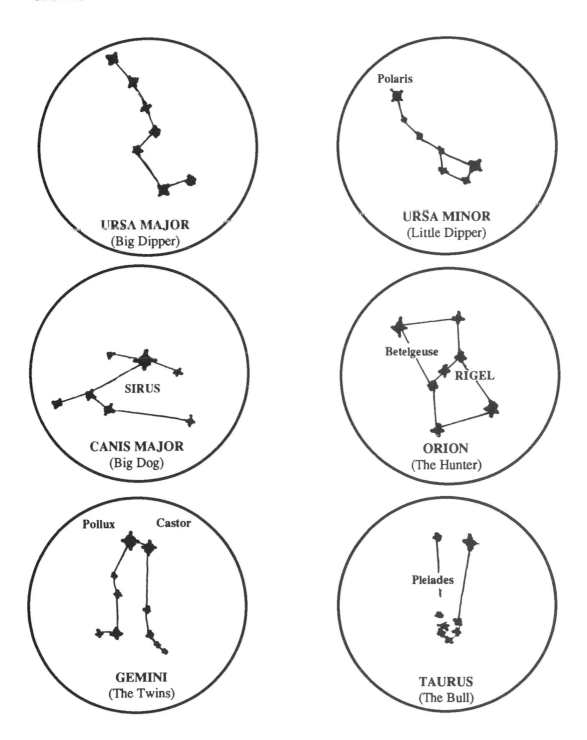

URSA MAJOR
(Big Dipper)

URSA MINOR
(Little Dipper)

Polaris

CANIS MAJOR
(Big Dog)

SIRUS

ORION
(The Hunter)

Betelgeuse

RIGEL

GEMINI
(The Twins)

Pollux   Castor

TAURUS
(The Bull)

Pleiades

Activity Two - **God Made the Moon**

The student follows the phases of the Moon through one complete cycle using the interactive poster described.

The student draws and colors the 'Man in the Moon' on a 16" by 16" square of white poster board. Be sure to leave spaces for the "eyes". These are 2 inch wide strips that slide through the cuts marked on the poster board. The student may also want to mark a calender as a diary of the Moon's phases.

Moon Phases Chart

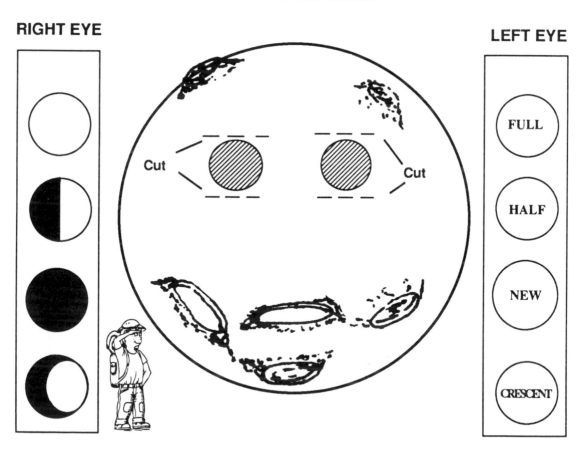

RIGHT EYE

LEFT EYE

"How many days does it take for the Moon to go from Full back to Full again?"

Activity Three - **What Time Is It? Ask the Sun!**

After the Biblical Flood people needed to keep track of time. Shadows cast by the Sun were an important way to record the hour of the day and the seasons of the year. Some of these ancient "watches" were impressive. Stone Henge in England is one example. The Nazca Lines in Peru are giant rock lines and images that follow the Sun's course over a year. Examples of these can be found in the library and shown to the student.

Have the student make a 2" by 4" by 3 feet wooden stake. Find a place in the yard where the Sun shines from noon throughout most of the afternoon. Place the stake so that a shadow is cast on the ground or fence.
The student makes a mark at the edge of the noon hour shadow and follows the shadow with markings every hour.

Over the next few days, have the student tell time by the shadow. When the shadow is between markings, the student should estimate.

Activity Four - **God Made the Seasons.**

To begin this activity, have the student collect pictures that represent the four seasons. A bulletin board or poster displaying the season's name and pictures may be made. **"What causes the seasons?" "Why is it cold in the winter?"**

Place a lamp with an exposed bulb on a desk or other raised platform. Make sure that the student can walk around the lamp unhindered. Take an orange and insert toothpicks halfway at the bottom and top of the orange.

The student tilts the plane of the toothpicks about 26 degrees from straight up and down. Explain that the Earth is tilted on the axis of its spin.

Have the student draw outlines of the continents on the orange with a black marker. (Be sure to include Australia.). Next place a dot approximately where the student lives. Place a dot in Australia.

Darken the room. With the toothpicks tilted at 26 degrees, have the student rotate the orange while standing still. **"When the Sun is shining on your home, is it also shining in Australia?"**

Now have the student move around the lamp <u>keeping the toothpicks tilted toward a stationary object in the room</u>. The half (top or bottom) of the orange closest to the "Sun" is in Summer.

As the student moves the Earth model around the "Sun", stop the student to ask if the season has changed. **"When it is summer in North America, what season is it in Australia?"**

Summer

Summer

INVESTIGATOR LEVEL

Activity Five - Follow That Star!

Now after Jesus was born in Bethlehem of Judea in the days of Herod the king, behold, magi from the east arrived in Jerusalem, saying, "Where is He who has been born King of the Jews? For we saw His star in the east, and have come to worship Him." Matthew 2: 1 -2.

As the Earth rotates, stars appear to move in the night sky. In this activity the student makes an astrolab -- a tool scientists use to chart the path of stars.

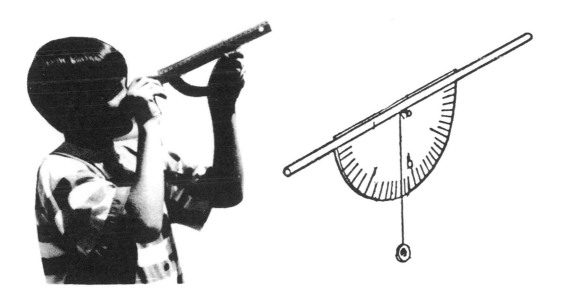

Tape a plastic protractor along the middle of a wooden ruler or other straight edged piece of wood. In the center of the protractor place a thumbtack and attach an eight inch length of thread. Tie a washer to the loose end of the thread.

The student will pick out a single star; for example, Betelgeuse. Site the star along the top edge of the ruler and try to hold the astrolab still to keep the washer from swinging. Have another student (or teacher) read the degrees on the protractor where the thread intersects. Record the result. Repeat the sighting and measurement an hour later. **"Has the position of the star changed?"**

If time allows observe move than one star. (**Polaris**, the North Star, located in the Little Dipper, is recommended.). **"Do all stars appear to move the same distance in the same amount of time?" "Are the stars really moving across the sky, or is the Earth moving, or both?"**

Activity Six - **The Heavens Declare the Glory of God.**

Page 85 shows the Summer and the Winter night skies of the Northern Hemisphere. One night have the student try to locate the major constellations shown on the star chart. (If a classroom project, this is an opportunity for parents to be involved.). In the constellation **Orion** are two well known stars. **Betelgeuse** (beatle' juice) is a star known as a red giant--if our Sun were a red giant, Earth would be in its outer edge! Betelgeuse is the star that makes Orion's left "shoulder". **Rigel** (rye' gel) is the bright star in Orion's right knee. Rigel is a blue-white star. Another constellation that follows Orion around the sky is **Canis Major**. In this constellation is found **Sirus**, also called the Dog Star. Sirus is a binary star, or two stars that orbit around each other, tied together by gravity.

Have the student try to locate the constellations mentioned in Job, chapter 38.

Summer Night Sky

Winter Night Sky

Activity Seven - Model of the Earth - Moon - Sun System.

An eclipse of the Sun is when the Moon in its orbit around the Earth comes between the Earth and Sun. Because the Moon is much closer to the Earth than the Sun, both the Moon and the Sun appear to be the same size! If you are in the right spot on Earth, a **total eclispe** of the Sun will occur. Observers in other places may see only a **partial eclispe**.

The phases of the Moon depends on how light from the Sun is blocked by the Earth. Give the student a flashlight, a card board disk the diameter of the the flashlight lens (the "Moon" disk), and another card board disk about 5 times as large as the "Moon " disk (the "Earth" disk). If time permits, have the student color both disks to look like the Earth and Moon.

Have the student develop and demonstrate a model that explains the phases of the Moon, and a total and partial eclispe of the Sun.

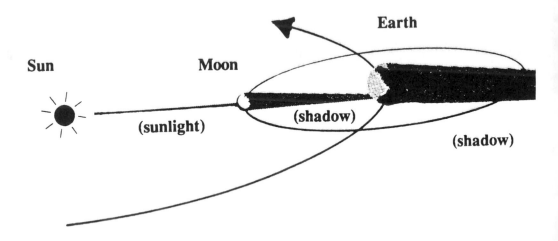

**RESEARCHER
LEVEL**

Activity Eight - A Tool to Observe the Heavens -- the Telescope.

The simple reflecting telescope diagrammed on the next page is not expensive. Through hands-on construction, the student will also learn principles of the reflecting telescope.

The 4 inch to 6 inch diameter cosmetic mirror is mounted in a plastic bowl of the same diameter. The hole cut in the bottom of a sturdy card board box should be slightly smaller than the diameter of the bowl. The objective is to make it possible to tilt the mirror-bowl system at different angles. To the top of the wooden upright--attached to the box by one wing nut and bolt--a smaller length of a wooden straight edge is attached by a second wing nut and bolt. Inexpensive binoculars or "spy" glass is attached by rubber bands. (If using binoculars, tape paper over one of the two oculars.).

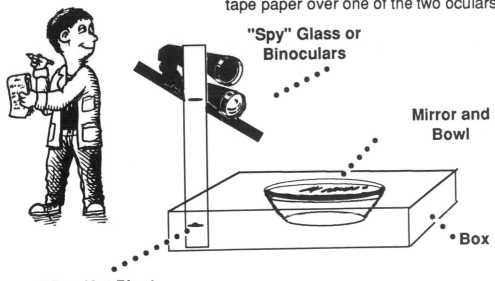

**"Spy" Glass or
Binoculars**

**Mirror and
Bowl**

Box

Wing Nut Pivot

Once constructed, the student should try focusing on the Moon by tilting the mirror-bowl system and adjusting the distance (focal distance) between the binoculars and the mirror. **"How does the Moon affect the Earth?"** One way is the effect that the Moon has on the ocean seen in ocean tides. Some scientist also believe that the Moon's gravity could trigger earthquakes, but this has not been proven. During its cycle from Full Moon back to Full Moon, the Moon's orbit is closest to the Earth at its **perigee**. In its **apogee** the Moon is furthest from Earth. **"Would the Moon effect ocean tides greater in apogee or perigee?"**

When successful, the student should be able to see individual craters. While observing the Moon, here are some questions to consider and discuss: **"What are the large dark areas of the Moon's surface called?" "When did the Moon get all of those craters?" "How would the Moon have looked before getting all those craters?"**

Maria was name by early astronomers who thought these dark areas on the Moon's surface might be seas or oceans. It now appears that the dark areas are where molten rock from inside the Moon broke onto the surface. The thousands of craters over the surface of the Moon are impressive. **"Why are there so many craters on the Moon and so few on Earth?'**

MARS VIKING ORBITER

EARTH LANDSAT

VENUS MARINER 2

SATURN VOYAGER 2

JUPITER PIONEER 11

Earth based telescopes are just one way we can look at objects in space. In 1991 the U.S. Postal Service issued a set of ten space exploration stamps. These stamps commemorate the knowledge gained through robot explorers such as the Mariner, Pioneer, and Voyager missions. **The student can collect these stamps and research the story behind each mission.**

Activity Nine - The Sun Has Spots?

**CAUTION
NEVER LOOK DIRECTLY AT THE SUN -- NOT WITH YOUR
EYE AND ESPECIALLY NOT THROUGH A TELESCOPE!**

Sunspots are giant magnetic storms that appear as dark spots on the Sun's surface. Scientists now know that sunspots are active in eleven year cycles. The most recent decline in sunspot activity began in 1980 and by 1985 there were almost none to be seen. 1990 was again a time for many sunspots.

Without looking at the Sun, the teacher and student can focus a telescope or pair of binoculars (with one side taped) on the sun by holding a white card over the eye piece. The Sun shining on the white card will show black dots if there is sunspot activity. If you observe the Sun during a period of high sunspot activity, repeat the observations over several days. The student may want to outline the sunspots on the white card showing their position at each observation. A new white card is used with each observation.

If the student knows a "ham" radio operator, have the student ask if sunspots affect their radio and in what ways. The interview could also be an opportunity for a research paper.

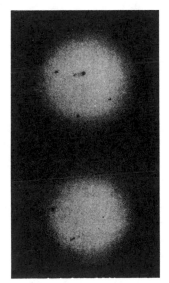

"How do the sunspots change over time?"

"In what ways can sunspots interact with Earth?"

Activity Ten - Sun, Atmosphere and the "Greenhouse Effect."

There is much talk about the "greenhouse effect." This activity demonstrates the effect.

Energy from the Sun is about 30 percent reflected by clouds, 20 percent absorbed by the atmosphere, and 50 percent absorbed by the Earth's surface.

The atmosphere has two important layers. The **troposphere** is the lowest layer where nearly all weather occurs. The **stratosphere** contains a gas call **ozone** that reacts with the harmful ultraviolet radiation portion of the light spectrum.

Light energy from the Sun enters the Earth's atmosphere and is absorbed as heat energy by the land and oceans and transformed into living materials (**biomass**) by organisms containing chlorophyll on the land and in the oceans. Some of the heat energy released by the land and reflected by bodies of water cannot travel back into space. Some gases, such as carbon dioxide, in the atmosphere help trap even more heat.

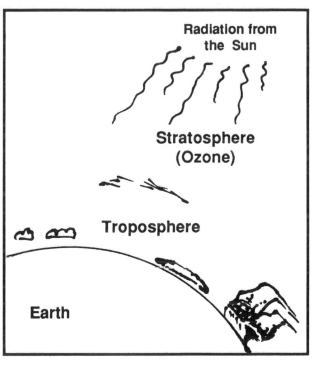

"What are some activities that release more carbon dioxide into the atmosphere?" (Examples include: destroying large areas of plants that change carbon dioxide into oxygen [rain forests]; burning fossil fuels in a way that releases carbon compounds into the atmosphere.).

The student can study two variable combinations at a time. For example, set up two pans of soil under the clear plastic and green plastic domes. The thermometers are set in the side of the domes about mid-way. Seal the thermometer in place with clay. Place the domes in sunlight. Take the temperature of the air outside the domes either before or after the experiment begins.

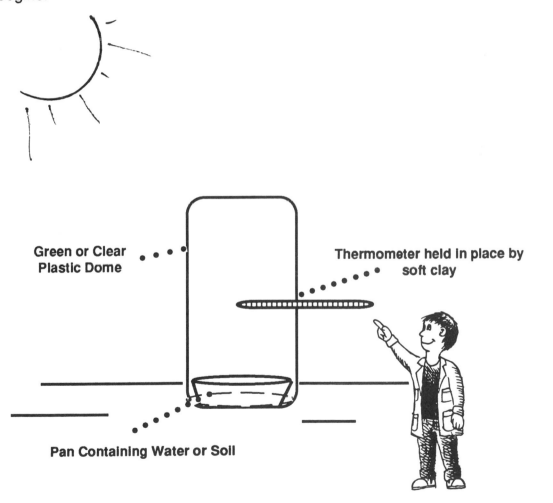

Green or Clear Plastic Dome

Thermometer held in place by soft clay

Pan Containing Water or Soil

The student will develop an experimental design with two variables as shown below. The combinations are:
   (a) temperature of air above a pot of soil with clear plastic dome;
   (b) temperature of air above a pot of soil with green plastic dome;
   (c) temperature of air above a bowl of water with clear plastic dome;
   (d) temperature of air above a bowl of water with green plastic
        dome; and
   (e) temperature of air outside the dome (room temperature).

The student can record results in a table:

	Green Plastic Dome	**Clear Plastic Dome**
Soil	Record Temperature Here	Record Temperature Here
Water	Record Temperature Here	Record Temperature Here

Temperature of air outside the domes _____.

"Is there any evidence that heat energy is trapped inside the domes?" "Is the air hotter trapped above the water or above the soil ?"

Who Am I?

(Below are clues from the life of a famous scientist. The scientist's identity is given on bottom of the References, page 132.)

As a small boy growing up in America, I always dreamed of on day travelling to the Moon.

When I completed college, I became a military pilot. I worked on a top secret airplane called the YF12A, which set speed and altitude records for the United States, but for many years I couldn't tell anyone, not even my own family.

Still, my big dream was to become an astronaut and go to the Moon. Finally, after being turned down two times, in April, 1966, NASA selected me for astronaut training. After more years of training I was selected to be part of the Apollo 15 mission to the Moon. At last the dream that I had as a small boy came true. I became one of only twelve people to walk on the Moon. This great adventure helped me praise the Creator who made the laws of science that make space travel possible. In my book, *Destination: Moon* I wrote, "With God in control of our lives, not only can we explore other planets, we have hope for this planet. With His help, you and I can have a part in making earth a better place for all of us. "

Since leaving NASA, I founded the High Flight Foundation and have made trips to Turkey in search of Noah's Ark.

Who am I?

NOTES

UNIT SIX

Birds and Sealife
Day Five of Creation

And God created the great sea monsters, and every living creature that moves, with which the waters swarmed after their kind, and every winged bird after its kind; ...And there was evening and there was morning, the fifth day.
Genesis 1: 21, 23.

God Created the Birds and Sealife

Learning Objectives

Explorer Level. The student will: -
* Identify animals that fly and their habitats;
* Identify and classify animals that live in water;
* examine design in a feather under magnification;
* Understand the concept of extinction.

Investigator Level. The student will: -
* Investigate feeding behavior in birds;
* Investigate nesting behavior in birds;
* Demonstrate the ability to construct an aquarium;
* Observe animal and plant populations in an aquarium;
* Understand the concept of food chains and food web.

Researcher Level. The student will: -
* Examine embryonic development in the chicken
* Survey an ecosystem;
* Understand the terms community, ecology, and ecosystem.

Materials Preparation

Explorer Level Activities. Resources for pictures of animals that fly which the student can use; useable resources for pictures of animals that live in water; access to pictures of extinct sealife; paper clips; magnet; string, stick; glue.

Investigator Level Activities. Popcorn; variety of fruits; variety of seeds; variety of nesting materials (thin paper strips, string, straw, thread, thin aluminium strips, etc.); an aquarium or clear plastic container about the size of a bread box; water plants; guppies; Daphnia; water snails; cardboard boxes; popsicle sticks.

Researcher Level Activities. Light bulb; newspaper and cardboard boxes; fertile hen or duck eggs; access to pond water; variety of glass containers; sugar, vinegar, salt, and ammonia; thermometer (Celsius or Fahrenheit); fresh fish-not cleaned, sharp knife; freshly killed chicken-defeathered, but not cleaned, sharp knife; glass container with screw-cap, small dead fish, pond mud and water.

Activities

Activity One - **Animals That Fly.**

The student collects cut-out pictures of animals that fly and places them on a poster or bulletin board. The teacher will make tags that say "Bird,"Reptile," "Mammal," and "Fish." The student can label animals as collected.

Have the student label the parts of a bird on page 99--and draw in the part that is missing!

Collect examples of feathers. Under a magnifier look at the design. **"Are all feathers designed the same?"**

Make a list of scriptures that mention birds--some will be excellent for the student to memorize (for example, Matthew 6:26).

Activity Two - **Animals That Live In Water.**
The student collects cut-out pictures of animals that live in water and places them on a poster or bulletin board. The teacher will make tags that say "Bird, "Reptile," "Mammal," and "Fish." The student can label animals as collected.

The student may label the parts of the fish on page 100.

Make a list of scriptures that mention animals that live in water. The student can identify the animals as bird, reptile, mammal, or fish. **Read Job 41: "What type of animal could Leviathan be?"** (*Dinosaurs Those Terrible Lizards* by Duane Gish is a very good reference for helping the student answer this question.).

Reference: **Dinosaurs Those Terriable Lizards**

Activity Three - **When Noah Went Fishing, What Did He Catch?**
The student may cut out or draw pictures of living and **extinct** creatures that live or lived in water. Since Creation, all creatures have lived with humans. Include such extinct animals as the marine dinosaurs. **"What happened to the dinosaurs?" "Why are so many of these animals no longer living?" "What does it mean to say an animal is extinct?"** (*Dinosaurs and the Bible* is an excellent reference to read to the student wanting a Biblical answer to these questions.).

Tape a paper clip to each of the cut-outs. Place the cut-outs in a large paper sack. Attach a magnet to a string from a dowel or short pole. Before the student puts the magnet "lure" in the bag, the class or teacher may say "Noah went fishing and what did he catch?" When the student brings the cut-out from the bag, he or she can identifiy the animal as reptile, fish, bird, or mammal; or by name; and whether or not the animal is still living or extinct.

Parts of the Bird

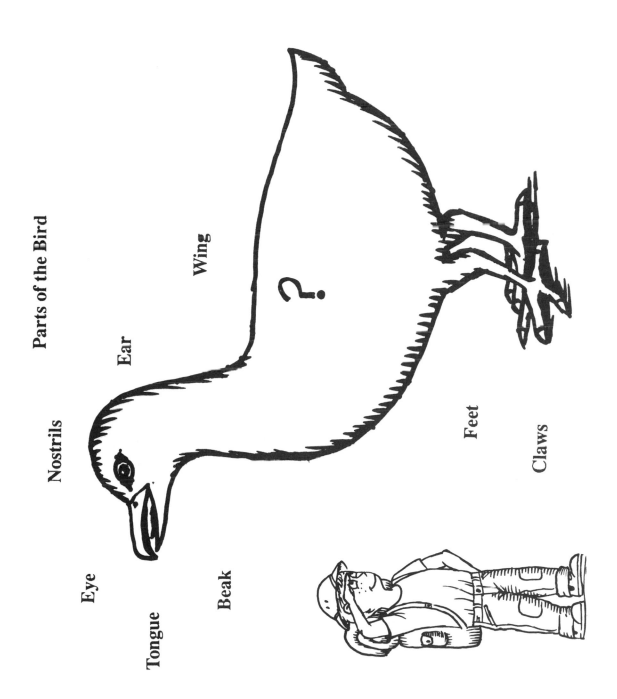

Wing

Ear

Nostrils

Eye

Tongue

Beak

Feet

Claws

Parts of the Fish

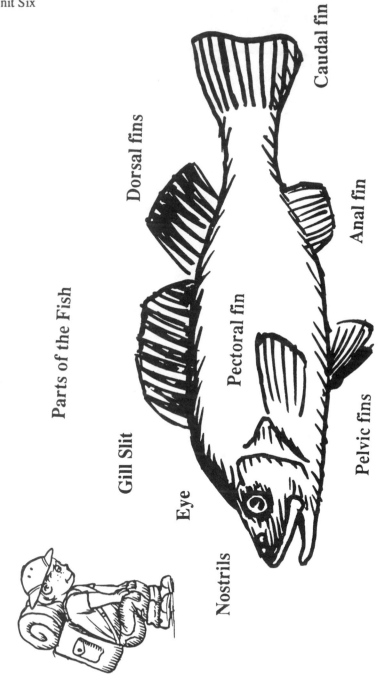

Dorsal fins

Caudal fin

Anal fin

Pectoral fin

Pelvic fins

Gill Slit

Eye

Nostrils

INVESTIGATOR LEVEL

Activity Four - **What Do Birds Like To Eat?**

In this activity the student will set up an experiment in bird behavior. Several different foods are threaded onto a string or stuck onto nails. The student observes which foods are being eaten and which birds (or other animals) are doing the eating.

Thread popcorn, a variety of seeds, lifesavers, cookies, (almost anything the student can imagine) onto a string. Try to tie the string onto a branch on which birds have been seen.

If the student or school has a yard with a fence (and is without cats) hammer 3 equally spaced nails through 2" by 4" by 1 -foot lengths of board that will rest (or can be attached) on the top fence support. Place different slices of foods, for example, different fruits or vegetables onto the nails.

Every other day the student should observe the experiment and record in the science notebook which foods are being eaten. Set aside a time for the student to observe what birds (or other animals) are eating and which foods they are eating. A elementary field book on birds (e.g., *Golden Book of Birds*) will be a useful aid to identification.

Activity Five - **What Do Birds Use For Nests?**

Usually, this activity is most successful in the early spring. The student acquires a small card board box, roughly 4'" by 4" by 4". Cut a hole about 2" diameter in the side of the box. Place materials in the box that birds may want to use for nests: for example, string, straw, cotton, strips of cloth, strips of wire, thin strips of aluminum foil--again almost anything that the student can imagine a bird might use to build a nest.

The student should count the number of each kind of nesting materials places in the box. Place the box in a tree and in an area protected from wind and rain.

For the following three days check the box daily. If nesting materials are not being taken then observe the box weekly. The student inventories the materials and notes which materials are missing. If possible ,observed the birds taking the nesting materials and try to locate their nests.

Activity Six - **Making and Observing an Aquatic Environment.**
        Environment is where animals and plants live. There are many different plants and animals that share the same environment. These living organisms are called a **community**. In this community are **primary producers**, such as plants that take nutrients from the soil and use sunlight to produce plant tissues that are food for other organisms in the community. In the aquatic environment, for example, small microscopic plants and animals called **plankton** are eaten by a variety of fish, shrimp, and crabs. These animals are eaten by larger fish or mammals such a otters and dolphins, which in turn, may be food for even larger animals. This chain of those organisms eating and being eaten is called a **food chain**. In the environment many food chains are linked to become a **food web**.
        Have the student make a food chain poster from cut-out pictures.
        To build an aquarium, the student needs a clear plastic container--about one gallon capacity. Add a layer of washed sand about 1 inch thick to the bottom of the container. When using tap water, allow the water to sit in the sun for at least a day before adding to the aquarium. Finally, add the water plants, daphnia, snails, and guppies. Have the student illustrate a food chain relationship for the aquarium on page 103.
        Cover the container with plastic wrap to reduce evaporation. Provide a light source (but insure that the temperature does not go over 80 degrees Fahrenheit).
        Determine a schedule with the student to make observations of the aquarium. Have the student record observations and drawings in his or her science notebook.

Draw the "food chain" of your aquarium's aquatic community.

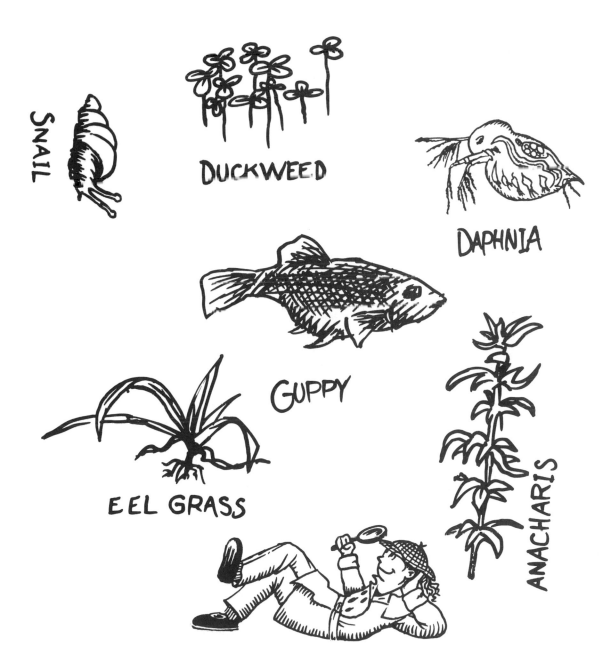

SNAIL

DUCKWEED

DAPHNIA

GUPPY

EEL GRASS

ANACHARIS

Activity Seven - Which Came First, the Chicken or the Egg?

Genesis answers that old question -- the chicken, and all other bird life, were created on the fifth Creation Day. But in this activity, the student will begin with the egg, and observe the embyronic development and hatching of a chick (or duckiling) by constructing an incubator.

Secure two cardboard boxes--the smaller one should hold about one dozen fertile eggs, light bulb, thermometer, and a small aluminum pan of water. The second larger box will hold this box with room to stuff waded newspapers in the gap between the smaller and larger box. The newspaper insulation can be varied to control temperature as can the wattage of the light bulb.

As diagrammed below, cut a small window that will be covered by glass. The window needs to be large enough to allow removal of eggs during the incubation process, but not too large to cause temperature fluctuations. The temperature inside the incubator needs to be a constant 103 degrees Fahrenheit for 21 days for complete incubation. Place a thermometer and pan of water inside the incubator. Observe the temperature though the window. When the temperature can be controlled to 103 degrees, place 10 fertile eggs in the incubator.

**Newspaper insulation
in space between boxes**

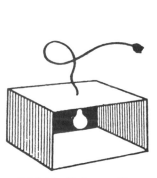

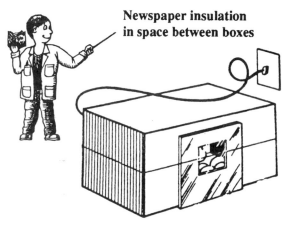

**Light bulb in smaller
box**

**Eggs, pan
of water,
thermometer**

Glass secured by twine

Every three days gently crack open an egg into a pan of water. After three days the chick embryonic heart beat can be observed. The student can record the development of the **embryo** through comments and drawings. Parallels between embryonic development of the chick can be made for other animals and humans. An excellent, Biblically sound presentation of human development and genetics for students is Dr. Gary Parker's book, *Life Before Birth* . It is highly recommended.

Some eggs should be allowed to incubate for the full 21 days. Once hatched, leave the chicks in an open box with the light source for warmth, sufficient water, and corn meal or commercially formulated chick feed. (You and the student will notice that the chicks or ducklings will imprint with humans once their eyes begin to focus in about seven days.).

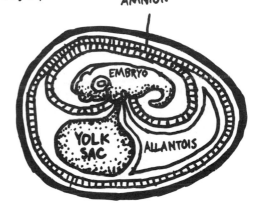

Twelve day embryo

Fourteen day embryo

Activity Eight - Changes in an Aquatic Community.

A field trip to a pond will provide an opportunity to observe a unique community. Have the student sit and quietly watch the activity. Record what is seen in the science notebook.

The student can be made aware of the often delicate balance that can exist in a small ecosystem. Pond water and a layer of bottom mud are collected in four glass containers. Cover the opening to three containers with gauze secured by a rubber band.   Seal one container with an air tight lid.

To one gauze covered container add four tablespoons of sugar -- the sugar represents sewage or waste water **pollution** dumped into a pond. Wrap the second in aluminum foil to reduce the amount of light available. The third container will be left as is. Place all four containers on a window sill--but not in direct sunlight.

Arrange a schedule with the student to observe the four containers. The student will record what changes are observed in each container over time. Typically, the "community" of organisms trapped in the containers will move from an **aerobic** (oxygen available) community to an **anaerobic** (oxygen not available) community of primarily bacteria (a black color typically results from anaerobic bacteria. The rate that the communities change will vary according to what was done to each container. The student will notice a change in odor as the pond **stagnates**.

| Air Tight Seal | Sugar Added | Control | Foil Wrapped |

Activity Nine - Dissecting a Fish.

Fish have been an important food source--even being identified as one of the meats that God allowed the children of Isreal to eat (Deut. 14:9, 10). Christ chose fishermen to be his disciples and made them, and now us, "fishers of men." (Mark 1:17). From that time until now, there have been people who have used the symbol of the fish to identify themselves as followers of Christ.

Christ created fish to serve as food, but he also gave us fish so that we might learn. Fish, as all other creatures, are designed uniquely for their habitats--and details of structure, function, and purpose in each animal, can tell us something about the Creator's Eternal Power and Glory (Romans 1).

A fresh fish can be preserved for a short period in isopropyl alcohol, available as "rubbing alcohol" in stores. Alcohol will dehydrate, or shrink, tissues and is not the best way to preserve specimens for long time periods.

Use a fish about 5 inches long--a size that can be easily stored in a lock seal food storage bag. The cut-away diagram on page 108 identifies the major internal parts of a fish. The external parts are identified on page 100. To dissect the student will use a sharp cuting tool, forceps (or tweezers), straight pins, and a piece of thick cardboard for laying the specimen onto and sticking the pins into.The student should be shown how to use an Exacto knife of safety-edge razor blade.

Some parts of the fish to identify are the **air bladder**, a thin sac that enables to fish to change depth in the water environment. Gases enter the sac from the bloodstream and leave the sac via the blood stream through the digestive system. The **gills** allow the fish to remove oxygen from water. Ocean dwelling fishes have the ability to excrete salt through specialized cells in the gills. Fish have a highly developed sense of smell using **olfactory sacs** behind each nostrils on its snout. Some scientists believe that migrating fish can find their way by the smell of plants in the water! Another unique design in the fish is how they hear. There are no external ears, but a **lateral line** down each side of the fish that can detect small changes in water current, underwater movements and pressure changes.

Have the student identify internal parts and research their purpose and function. This activity can provide an opportunity for an oral presentation by the student.

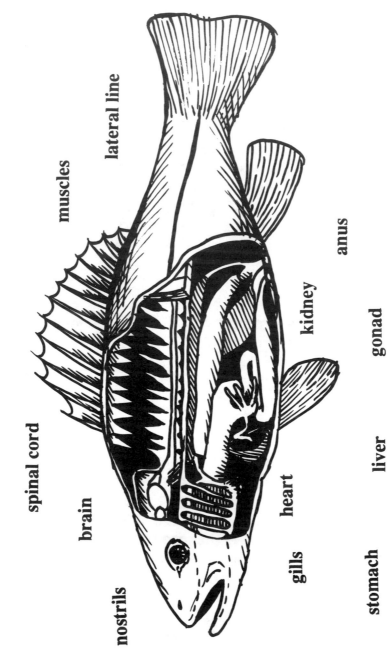

lateral line

muscles

air bladder

spinal cord

brain

nostrils

anus

kidney

gonad

liver

heart

gills

stomach

Internal Anatomy of the Fish

Activity Ten   **- Dissecting a Bird or a Dinosaur?**
It is <u>not</u> true that your Thanksgiving turkey is really a dinosaur. It is popular for evolutionist--people who believe that all living creatures came from a ball of slime millions of years ago--to teach that birds came from dinosaurs.

A fossil that has been claimed to be part bird and part dinosaur is ***Archaeopteryx*** (ark e OPT tricks). This fossil shows bird feathers and wings, but there are also characteristics of reptiles--teeth and wing claws. But there are birds living today with some of these characteristics; for example, the young hoatzin of South America uses its wing claws to climb trees. Like living birds, the fossils also show that the living *Archaeopteryx* was probably a strong flyer. **Have the student examine a feather under a magnifier. Observe the design.**

Another blow to the idea that *Achaeopteryx* is part dinosaur and part bird came with the recent discovery of more bird fossils that are like modern bird skeletons. Both birds, *Archaeopteryx* and modern-type birds, lived at the same time. If you believe the Bible, this is not surprising. **"What two birds did Noah release from the Ark?"**

An animal that has physical characteristics found in other, unrelated animals is called a **melange**. The platypus is an example. Have the student research the platypus. **"What designs in the platypus are found in other animal groups?" "How does the platypus use its unique design?"**

Locate a poultry processor (or farmer) that can supply freshly killed chickens that have not been cleaned.   With adult supervision, have the student remove the digestive tract. Birds have high body temperatures, and those that fly have an extremely high demand for energy. The digestive system in birds is designed for eating large amounts of food and digesting it quickly. A bird's bill or beak is a specialized tool for acquiring food. Birds do not chew their food--they swallow it whole. The **crop** stores the food until it can pass into a two-part stomach. Fhe first part of the stomach produces digestive juices. The second part is the thick-walled **gizzard**. Have the student open the gizzard and describe the contents. The gizzard grinds the food against sand and stones that are also eaten by the bird for this purpose. The digestive system of a bird is shown on page 110.

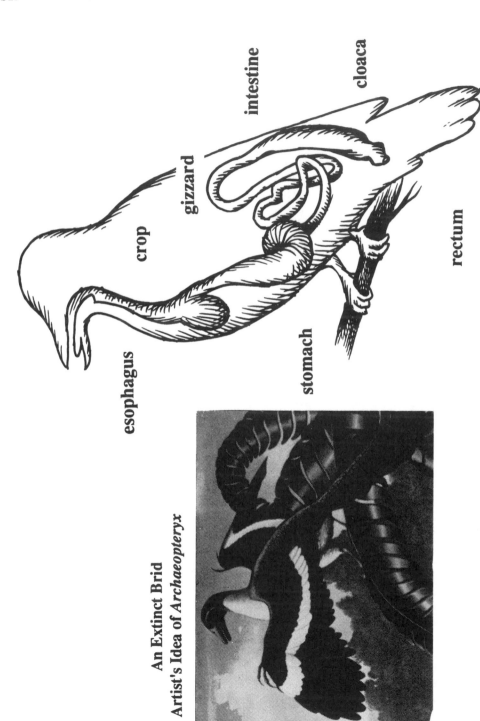

Digestive System of the Bird

esophagus

crop

gizzard

intestine

cloaca

rectum

stomach

An Extinct Brid
Artist's Idea of Archaeopteryx

Activity Eleven - **Fossil or Yuk: Studying Decomposers in the Aquatic Habitat.**

How are fossils made? The study of how fossils are made is called **taphonomy** (TAFF on o me).

Most textbooks tell a story about an animal that died in a swamp, and how over time sediment (mud) buried the dead animal. Eventually, the animal was completely buried and pressure from above of more mud, along with minerals dissolved in the mud, combined to turn the dead animal's skeleton into rock - a **fossil**.

The science of taphonomy has shown that fossils are not made in this way. In fact, the best conditions for turning a dead animal into a fossil requires **sudden burial with lots of mud**--conditions produced by the Biblical Flood. When visiting an ocean beach, how many bivalve seashells (clams, oysters, or scallops) do you see that are closed with the animal still inside? Not many--most shells are open or with one half missing. That is because when the animal dies, the muscle no longer holds the two shell halves together. It is then attacked by **scavengers** or starts to decay. When you look at fossil bivalve shells, many occur whole--both halves are together. **"What does this say about how the animal died and how fast it was buried?"**

Fill a glass container (with a screw-on cap) with pond mud. Add pond water to finish filling the container. Take a small dead fish (guppie or gold fish; we've found pet stores usually have a daily supply) and place it in the glass container--about half-way down into the mud and next to the glass wall so that the fish can be easily seen. Seal the container.

Observe the dead animal over a several months. Have the student keep a log of what he observes.

Because of **decomposers**, primarily bacteria, in the container, the fish decays. In aquatic ecosystems microorganisms play an important role. **"How does decomposition help in an aquatic habitat?" "How could decomposition make the habitat unsuitable for some living organisms?" "Is the glass container, with mud and the dead fish, a closed or open system?" "Is the dead fish becoming a fossil?"**

The student can set-up other containers using dead plants or other small animals and compare observations.

Who Am I?

(Below are clues from the life of a famous scientist. The scientist's identity is given on bottom of the References, page 132.)

Although scholars call me the father of glacial geology (the science of glaciers) my studies on fish, both living and fossil, have never been equaled.

I taught in Europe and in America. While in Switzerland, my studies of Alpine glaciers led me to the idea of the Pleistocene Ice Age, which most creationists believe to be the only real epoch of the so-called "geological ages."

My classes taught at Harvard in natural history were said to have produced all the outstanding teachers of that subject in America during the last half of the 19th Century. I established the Museum of Comparative Zoology while at Harvard, which has been named in my honor.

I was the son of a preacher and descended from a long line of clergymen. I believed in God. I also believed that He made every kind of plant and animal by the power of His Word, and that He made them to reproduce after their own kind. This is known as Special Creation. Because I had knowledge of more animals, living or fossil, than the other scientists of my time, I remained a strong opponent of evolution throughout my life.

Who am I?

Reference: *Men of Science/Men of God* by H. Morris. 1988.

UNIT SEVEN
Land Animals and Humans Day Six of Creation

And God made the beasts of the earth after their kind, and the cattle after their kind, and everything that creeps on the ground after its kind; and God saw that it was good. Then God said, "let Us make man in Our image, according to Our likeness; and let them rule over the fish of the sea and over the birds of the sky and over the cattle and over all the earth and over every creeping thing that creeps on the earth." - Genesis 1: 25 - 26.

God Created the Land Animals and Humans

Learning Objectives

Explorer Level. The student will: -
* Understand that God created all animals, including the dinosaurs;
* Understand what science can know and what God has revealed about dinosaurs;
* Make and observe animals in a terrarium;
* Conduct a survey of a habitat;
* Understand and use the term habitat;
* Make an interactive model of what it may have been like in Noah's time.

Investigator Level. The student will: -
* Understand what science can know and what God has revealed about dinosaurs and apply to other areas of science;
* Conduct experiments in isopod behavior;
* Understand the uniqueness of God's creative design in the lowly isopod;
* Construct and draw to scale an interactive model of the human skeletal, nervous, digestive, endocrine and circulatory systems;

Researcher Level. The student will: -
* Experiment with how animals are designed by God to respond to their environment;
* Model osmosis in the cell.

Materials Preparation

Explorer Level Activities. Children's Bible; pictures of Apatasaurus (Brontosaurus), hippopotomus, and elephant; 1 gallon clear plastic container, sand, rocks, isopods or crickets; habitat board (half inch thick board at least two foot square); cardboard box, popsicle sticks, cut-outs of extinct plants and animals, 3 - 4 small magnets, paper clips.

Investigator Level Activities. Isopods (rolly pollies, cow bugs); 1 gallon clear plastic container, sand, 2 four inch squares of cardboard; butcher paper the length of the student's body, colored marking pens;

Researcher Level Activities. Cardboard box, plastic wrap, thermometer (Celsius or Fahrenheit), cricket; bowl of ice, lamp, aluminum square cake pan, black marker, ruler, plastic wrap, variety of insects; 10 wooden stakes and twine; 2 liter clear plastic soft drink bottle, plastic sandwich bag, thick syrup, twist tie.

Activities

**EXPLORER
LEVEL**

Activity One - God Made the Dinosaurs.
Read the description of the animal that God revealed to Job in Chapter 40: 15 - 24. Have pictures of a hippopotomus, elephant, and apatasaurus (brontosaurus) on a poster. Place clues under each animal as the student associates the clue with the animal(s). The clues may be as follows:

    vs. 15 -- eats grass like an ox;
    vs. 16 -- strength in its hind legs, and powerful
                 muscles in its abdomen (belly);
    vs. 17 -- tail bends like a cedar tree;
    vs. 18 -- bones are like tubes of metal;
    vs. 19 -- largest of all God's creatures;
    vs. 23 -- if a river floods, it is not concerned;
    vs. 24 -- no one can capture it when it is watching.

Reference: **Dinosaurs and the Bible** by D. Unfred. 1990.

Activity Two - **Observing Land Animals in a Terrarium.**
   Place a layer of pebbles or small rocks in a one gallon clear plastic container. Add a one to two inch layer of soil. The student can plant and lightly water seeds in the terrarium at this time. Add isopods (rolly pollies, sow bugs) and or crickets. Cover the terrarium with screen mesh folded and stapled into the shape of a lid or a piece of heavy cardboard with small holes punched in it.
   The student and teacher will establish a time that the terrarium is to be observed. Observing changes in a terrarium can be a semester long project. Concepts such as that of a food chain (**Which are the eaters?"** and **"Which are being eaten?"**) can now be introduced. Drawings and verbal observations can be reported. **"What has changed in the terrarium?" "Is anything different?"**
   If it's a time of year that caterpillars are active, you may want to substitute them in the terrarium temporarily. Leaves and stems of the plant that the caterpillars are eating should be added to the terrarium. This is an excellent opportunity to observe stages of **metamorphosis**.
   "How do insects grow?" (Expect observed responses such as the shedding of their skin, coat, outer layer, etc.)
   Add a spider to the terrarium. The student can observe **predator - prey** relationships in the food chain.

Activity Three - **Observing Animals in Their Habitat.**
   The student selects an area (outside) to study. A lawn, pasture, wooded area are all possibilities, and this activity can be repeated so that the student explores different habitats.
   The student places the habitat board on the ground. The board is left undisturbed for 3 to 4 days (or longer). The student will turn over the board and record verbally or through drawing which animals and animal activities (e.g., burrrowing) are observed. **"How would you describe the habitat under the habitat board?" "What organisms are living in this habitat?" "What are the organisms doing?"**

Activity Four - What Did A Tyrranosaurus Eat?

Students have seen pictures of the *Tyrranosaurus Rex* --the Terrible King Lizard. Ask the student what tyrranosaurus ate, and the majority would probably say meat or other dinosaurs or "Just about anything it wanted to!". **"How do you know what a tyrranosaur ate?"**

In this activity students will be made aware of the difference between the imagination of scientists and historical revelation from God. Most people believed that tyrranosaurs were meat eaters because of the long, pointed dagger-like teeth found with the fossil.

The picture of the monkey on page 118 shows long canine teeth. This animal is not a predator, but a fruit eater. **"What do you think the monkey eats with his long sharp teeth?"**

Recent studies have shown that the teeth of the tyrranosaurs had shallow roots. After providing this new information to the student ask, **"What would happen if a tyrranosaur bit into a galloping five ton triceratop?"** The tyrranosaur would probably lose a few of his best teeth! Have the student draw what they think the tyrranosaur ate. (Any response is acceptable--including ripe juicy melons!). When the tyrranosaur was first created, it and all other animals were **herbivores**--plant eaters, not meat eating **carnivores**.

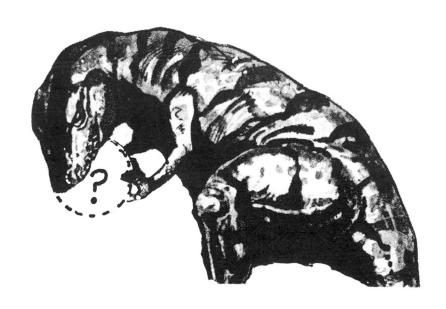

What Did *Tyrannosaurus* Eat?

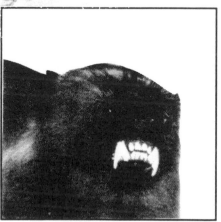

What big teeth! What does this monkey eat?

Reference: **Dinosaurs and the Bible** (1990).

**INVESTIGATOR
LEVEL**

Activity Five - **What Was It Like When Noah Lived?**
The strange, long dead, animals that we piece together from fossil bones were living when Noah was building the Ark. In this activity, the students are encouraged to draw and cut-out pictures of extinct animals. The student should read the story of Noah and his preparation for the worldwide Flood catastrophe.

Have the student tell a story using the "dinorama" described on the next page. Paper clips are taped to the back of the cut-out animals. Small magnets are glued or taped onto popsicle sticks. By moving the popsicle stick-magnet under the "stage" or behind the "backdrop" the student (or students) can act out his story of life with Noah.

Dinorama

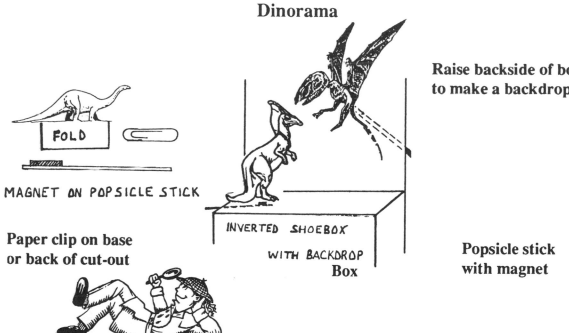

MAGNET ON POPSICLE STICK

**Raise backside of box
to make a backdrop**

**Paper clip on base
or back of cut-out**

**Popsicle stick
with magnet**

An imaginary story of life before the Flood based on Biblical history and science discoveries has been written by Dr. Ruth Beechick, titled **Adam and His Kin**. This book would be excellent for a story time and generate some ideas for the student's own presentation.

Activity Six - **Crabs and Isopods.**
Crabs, lobsters, and crayfish are crustaceans that live in a water environment. But the lowly isopod, also called a rolly polly, pill bug, or sow bug is a **crustacean** too. Even though they live on land, isopods have platelike gills along their lower underside or **abdomen**. Isopods must have moisture to breathe.
Have the student examine a dead isopod with a hand lens. **"Can you find the isopod's gills?"** **"How do living isopods react when bothered?"** **"What other animals act this way when disturbed?"**
Place a dry paper towel and a moist paper towel in a box with isopods. Leave overnight. The next day have the student lift the two towels. **"Which environment did the isopods prefer?"**

Activity Seven - **A Segmented Worm.**
Almost everyone has seen an earthworm--some students have probably used them for fishing. It is easy for us to overlook God's design and purpose in creatures such as these. Scientists now know that the benefits resulting from the activities of these creatures is almost beyond calculation.
The earthworm eats soil. The soil contains decaying plant and animal tissue which provides food for the earthworm. The soil eating also enriches and improves the soil. The earthworm burrows make it easier for water and oxygen to get into the soil. Decaying materials that provide nitrogen and minerals for plant roots are mixed in the soil because of the worm's activities. One earthworm will produce a half pound of rich, fertile soil in one year.
Have the student prepare an aquarium or plastic bin by placing an inch inch thick layer of small rocks over the bottom. Next, lay down a 4-inch layer of garden soil. On top of this layer add crumpled dried leaves and grass clippings. Cover this layer with another four inches of garden soil.
Go exploring for earthworms (or save the ones that you found digging in the garden). Place the earthworms in the aquarium. Have the students observe and describe their burrowing activity.
Keep the soil moist with a spray bottle of water. Caution: Wet soil will drown the earthworms. Have the student keep a log of the earthworms activities throughout the semester. At the end of the semester clean out the bin. **"Have the number of worms increased?"**

Activity Eight - Inside the Human Body.

Give the student a sheet of butcher paper that is as long as the student is tall. For this activity the student should wear long pants. Have the student lie down on the paper with his head to one side. The teacher or another student will draw an outline of the student onto the paper. The student can fill in the eyes, nose, mouth, and the skeletal system.

Using the patterns on pages 122 and 126, the student will use other paper to draw and color the organs of the digestive, respiratory, endrocrine, circulatory, and nervous systems. Have the student also reference these systems in an encyclopedia.

The student can tape (or use tacky, non-permanent glue) the different systems onto their own body outline. Have the student give an oral report on each body system.

Activity Nine - Experimenting To Discover How Animals Interact With Their Environment.

Animal behavior does not happen by accident. God has designed animals so that by studying them we can see His handiwork in Creation.

For example, the tree cricket is so sensitive to temperature that it acts like a living thermometer! The number of chirps that this cricket makes in 15 seconds plus 39 equals the temperature in degrees Fahrenheit. Inside the cricket is a complex life chemistry, or **biochemistry,** that enables the organism to survive and reproduce. The biochemistry that causes the cricket to chirp is closely regulated by temperature.

In this activity the student will experiment with temperature and cricket chirping. Take any box that can be sealed. Cut a view window in one side of the box. Cover the window with plastic wrap. Put a thermometer in the box so that it can be seen through the view window. Place a cricket in the box. At different times during the day count the number of chirps in 15 seconds. Add 39 to this number. How does this compare with the temperature in the box?

Skeletal System

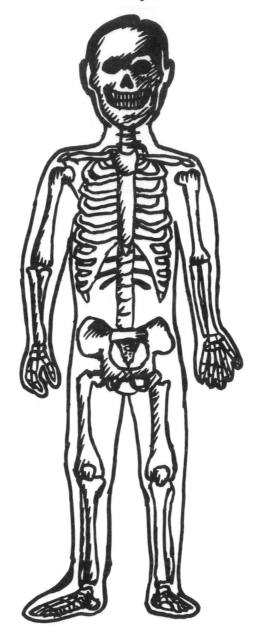

How Many Bones Do You Know?

Circulatory System

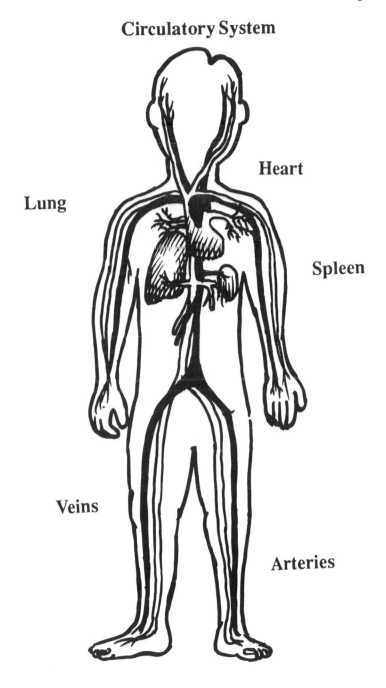

Heart

Lung

Spleen

Veins

Arteries

Nervous System

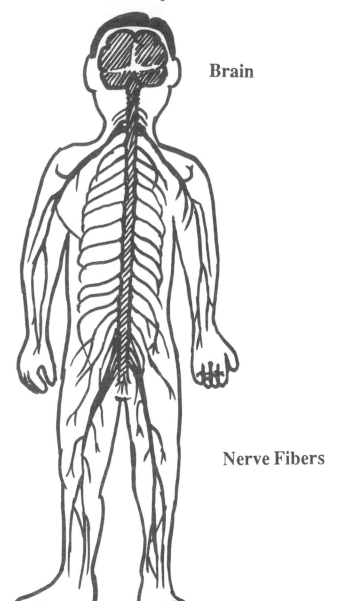

Brain

Spinal Cord

Nerve Fibers

Endrocrine System

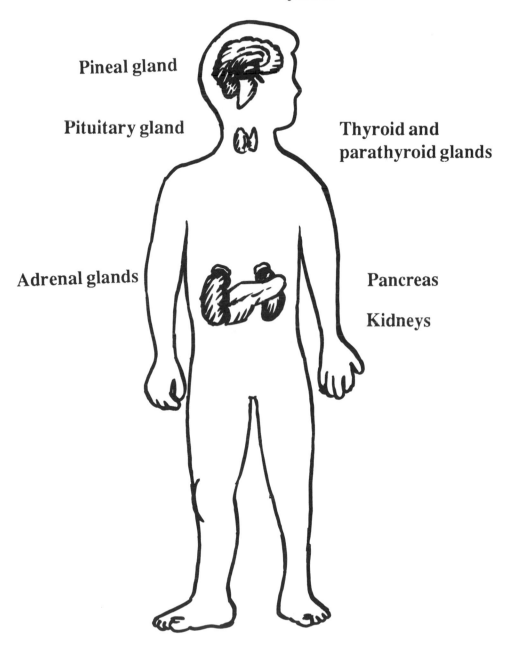

Pineal gland

Pituitary gland

Thyroid and
parathyroid glands

Adrenal glands

Pancreas

Kidneys

Digestive System

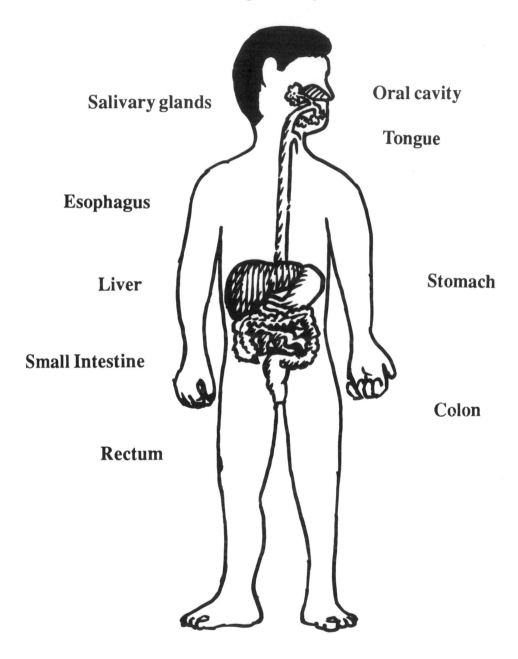

Salivary glands

Oral cavity

Tongue

Esophagus

Liver

Stomach

Small Intestine

Colon

Rectum

**RESEARCHER
LEVEL**

Activity Ten - **Studying How Animals Respond To Temperature.**

This experiment requires that the student collect a number of insects (or isopods). Caterpillars and isopods are easiest to use, but ants and other insects are successful substitutes.

The student marks an aluminum cake pan in a grid pattern described below. One end of the pan is placed on a bowl of ice. The opposite end is placed over a lamp so that the bottom of the pan is heated by the bulb.

Holding the thermometer on the middle of each grid, the student determines the temperature. Once the **temperature gradient** is determined between the hot and cold ends of the pan, place the insects (6 to 10) in the middle of the pan, cover and seal with plastic wrap. Allow 30 minutes to one hour.

"How many insects are in each grid?" "Which grid has the most insects?" "Does more than one kind of insect prefer the same grid temperature?" "What temperature is most preferred?"

Top view of pan showing grid pattern. The temperature is taken on the middle of each grid.

Lamp

Ice bowl or bucket

Activity Eleven - The Energy Pyramid.

Ecology is the study of how plants and animals--all organisms--relate to their environment and to each other. In the beginning, before Adam and Eve sinned, animals and humans just ate plants, not each other. After sin allowed death to enter Creation a whole new order of relationships came into being.

The energy pyramid shown below describes how energy flows through the environment. The pyramid shape suggests that the plants and animals at the bottom of the pyramid (the producers) are more numerous than the animals at the top of the pyramid (the carnivores). Scavengers and decomposers can interact with all levels of the energy pyramid.

Have the student collect pictures and make a poster of organisms that fit into each of these categories. Have the student explain how energy from the sun in cycled throughout the energy pyramid in the environment.

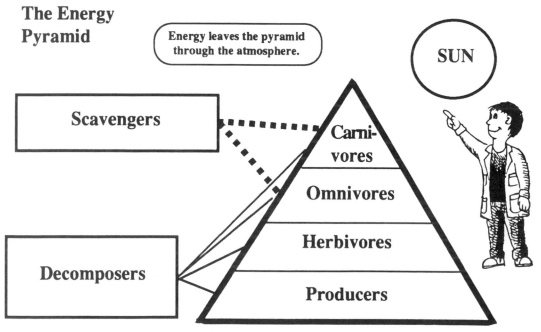

The Energy Pyramid

Energy leaves the pyramid through the atmosphere.

SUN

Scavengers

Carni-vores

Omnivores

Herbivores

Decomposers

Producers

Definations. **scavenger** - animal feeding on dead animals; **decomposer** - microbe or small animal that causes or assists in the break-down of dead plants and animals; **omnivore** - animal that eats both plants and animals; **carnivore** - animal that eats other animals; **herbivore** - animal that eats only plants; producer - any organism that produces its own food.

Activity Twelve - Surveying a Small Community.

Ecologists, scientists who study ecology, use many different methods to find out what organisms and how many live in a particular habitat. One method is called the **line transect survey**.

In this method a length of string is laid-out in a straight line arcoss the ground. The string is sixty feet long and is marked with a colored marking pen every three feet. Kite string is recommended. The string is anchored on each end by a large nail or wooden stake.

The student identifies, counts, and records any plant that the line crosses over. Any animals that cross under the line (such as insects), or cross over the line (such as larger animals, flying insects, and birds) are also identified and counted. The student can collect specimens of plants (or insects) to identify later using field guides. (Any library usually has an assortment of field guides for this purpose.).

The student prepares a data sheet like the one described below on which to record results. The student records results using a symbol, a drawing, or name to identify the plant or animal observed and counted.

Have the student evaluate this method of surveying a small community. **"Was the survey a good way to find out what was in this living community?" "What were some of the problems?" "Can you think of a better way of surveying a community of plants and animals?"**

Data Sheet for Recording Line Transect Survey Results

1	2	3	4	5	6	7	8	9	10	11	12	13	14	15	16	17	18	19	20

Use this space to record identification and number of animals in each grid.

Use this space to record identification and number of plants in each grid.

Each numbered grid represents 3-feet of string.

Activity Thirteen - Inside the Cell.

In our bodies cells are organized into tissues, and tissues are organized into organs and structures. So complex is its design that much of what happens in the cell is still a mystery.

The student may label the cell diagram below. One important part of the cell is its wall. The **cell wall** sometimes acts like a gate. It can selectively allow substances to travel between the inside of the cell and the environment outside the cell. One way that the cell interacts with the environment is by a process called **osmosis**.

The student places a thick syrup into a plastic sandwich bag which is sealed with a twist tie. Suspend the syrup-containing bag in a container of pure water--preferrably a container that the student can see through. The student observes what happens over the class period and again on the following day. **"What changes occurred inside the bag?" "What changes occurred outside the bag?" "How would you explain what happened and why it happened?"**

Inside the Cell

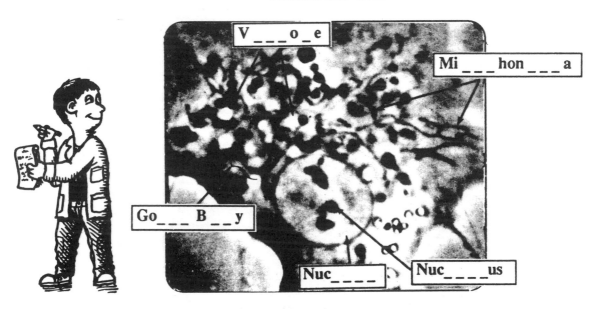

V _ _ _ o _ e

Mi _ _ _ hon _ _ _ a

Go _ _ _ B _ _ y

Nuc _ _ _ _

Nuc _ _ _ _ us

The Cell

Who Am I?

(Below are clues from the life of a famous scientist. The scientist's identity is given on bottom of the References, page 132.)

I am widely known as the father of biological taxonomy--the classification of plants and animals.

Throughout my life I had great respect for the Bible. In the book of Genesis we are told that God created the plants and animals to reproduce after their own kind. What was meant by the word "kind?" Finding an answer to this question became one of my main goals in life.

As a creationist, I believed that whatever the concept of kind meant, it certainly did not mean that one animal could evolve into a totally different kind of animal--or plant for that matter. I firmly believed in "fixity of species" and was, in fact, the scientist who first used the term *species* , which in Latin means--as you can probably guess--kind.

I never succeeded in defining what was meant by the Biblical word "kind." That mystery I will leave for other creation scientists in the future. Since it is a historical fact that all animals that exist today had ancestors on Noah's Ark, perhaps that might be a good place to begin. You just might be the scientist to solve this problem.

Who am I?

Reference: *Men of Science/Men of God* by H. Morris. 1988.

Selected References

The following references will enrich any science program and are some of the best creation science resources available.

Adam and His Kin by Ruth Beechick. 1990. Arrow Press. (All grades).
   Dr. Beechick creates a historical fiction of the world before the Genesis using Biblical, archeological, and scientific resources.
Destination: Moon by Jim Irwin. 1990. Multnoma Press. (All grades).
   An account of Col. Irwin's preparation to travel to and explore the moon's surface.
Dinosaurs and the Bible by David Unfred. 1990. Huntington House. (All grades).
   Dinosaurs--from discovery of the first fossils to the current search for living dinosaurs are documented in this book. Historical catastrophes and the greatest catastrophe of all, the Genesis Flood, are described.
Dry Bones and Other Fossils by Gary Parker. 1985. Master Books. (Grades 4 - 6).
   The best introduction to the study of fossils and how they were (and are) formed.
God Created the Birds ; **God Created the World**; **God Created Sealife** by Snellenberger. 1989. Master Books. (Grades 1 - 3). A collection of color sticker books with excellent content.
Men of Science/Men of God by Henry Morris. 1988. Master Books. (Grades 5 to Adult). This book gives short biographies of over 100 famous scientists.
Mystery of Early Man and the Bible by David Unfred. (1992, in press). Didaskon Publishing. (All grades). What about cavemen and the Ice Age? This book looks at science and Biblical history from the time the Ark landed to the time of Job--the book of the Bible that describes life after the Flood.
Voyage to the Stars by Richard Bliss. 1991. Institute for Creation Research. (Grades 5 - High School). An introduction to astronomy.
Unlocking the Mysteries of Creation by Dennis Petersen. 1986. CEI. (All Grades). A mine-encyclopedia of the evidences for Biblical Creation.

Who Am I? answers: Unit Two, page 28 - **Isaac Newton** (1642 - 1727); Unit Three, page 50 - **Matthew Maury** (1806 - 1873); Unit Four, page 74 - **Robert Boyle** (1627 - 1691); Unit Five, page 94 - **James Irwin** ; Unit Six, page 112 - **Louis Agassiz** (1807 - 1873); Unit Seven, page 131 - **Carolus Linneaus** (1701 - 1778).

Selected Vocabulary

Acid - Any substance that gives off hydrogen ions in water or neutralizes a base.

Aerobic - Life that grows only in air.

Air - The mixture of gases in the atmosphere.

Air Pressure - The pressure caused by weight of the gases in the atmosphere above us.

Allantois - A membrane in the egg of birds and reptiles.

Amnion - A clear membrane in the egg of birds and reptiles.

Anaerobic - Life that grows only in the absence of air.

Apogee - When the Moon's orbit is farthest away from Earth.

Artery - A blood vessel carrying blood away from the heart.

Astronomy - The study of the universe.

Atmosphere - The blanket of air surrounding the earth.

Atom - The smallest unit in which an element may exist. Elements may also exist in compounds and molecules.

Average - A math tool from a tool kit called statistics. The average is the sum of the variable data divided by the total number of variables.

Barometer - A tool for measuring air pressure.

Barometic Pressure - Air pressure measured by a barometer.

Base - A substance that neutralizes an acid.

Battery - A chemical storage cell that can be made to produce a flow of electrons in a closed circuit.

Binary Star - Two stars that orbit around each other--Sirius is an example.

Biochemistry - Chemistry of living things.

Bio mass - The total of living material in a selected area or habitat.

Capillary tubes - Small tubes of plant tissue that draw water upwards to other parts of the plant.

Carbon dioxide - One of the gases in the atmosphere. God designed plants to "breath" this gas and release back into the atmosphere oxygen--the gas that animals breath.

Carnivore - A plant or animal that eats animals; e.g., plant carnivore - Venus fly trap.

Cell - The smallest organized unit in a living system.

Cell Wall - The wall around the cell.

Cell Membrane - The envelope next to the cell wall that protects the contents of the cell and selectively transports substances between the cell and its outside environment.

Chemical reaction - When two or more compounds react together to produce a new set of compounds called products.

Chlorophyll - The green pigment in plants required for photosynthesis--the combining of carbon dioxide and water to form plant tissue using light energy.

Chloroplast - Special cells in the plant containing chlorophyll--the green pigment that lets the plant use light energy from the Sun.

Chromatogram - When substances are separated by the tool chromatography, a chromatogram is produced.

Community - A group of living organisms living in a specific habitat.

Compound - A substance made of two or more elements in specific proportions.

Closed system - Any system that cannot exchange freely with the surrounding environment.

Condensation - When gas changes into a liquid state--as water vapor condenses to form water droplets.

Constellations- Groups of stars that have been given a special meaning by men or by God.

Crater - A cuplike depression surrounding a volcano or hole resulting from the impact of a chunk of space rock.

Crystal - A solid with a regular geometric pattern or design.

Data - Measurements recorded by a scientist.

Decomposer - Any bacteria, protozoa, or small animal that helps to break-down dead plant and animal tissue.

Depth - A vertical (up-down) measurement.

Dicotyledon - A seed with two halves.

Eclipse - When a body in space passes between the observer and another body.

Ecology - The study of how plants and animals relate to their environment.

Element - The smallest whole unit of matter composed of one or more neutrons, protons and electrons.

Embryo - The early stage of development in the life of an organism.

Environment - A living organism's surroundings.

Energy - The ability to do work.

Energy pyramid -The concept that energy from the Sun or environment passes through different organisms, with the producers being at the bottom of the pyramid and different types of consumers on top.

Evaporation - The process of water molecules in liquid form moving into the air as a gaseous form.

Fahrenheit - A scale for measuring temperature.

Fiber optics - A system using glass fiber to move light over great distances.

Food chain - The sequence that food travels in a habitat or ecosystem.

Food web - The complex pattern of linked and overlapping food chains in an ecosystem.

Fossil - Impression, cast, or mineralized part of the body of a dead animal or plant.

Freezing point - The temperature at which liquid water turns to ice (solid).

Gas - State of matter where the molecules are far enough apart to exist as a cloud or vapor.

Germination - The growth of a seed.

Golgi body - A small unit (organelle) within the cell that assembles and packages proteins for use by the cell.

Graph - A visual picture of data.

Gravity - Most significantly, the force pulling objects toward the Earth. All objects have gravity.

Greenhouse effect - When the Sun's heat is trapped and accumulates in the atmosphere.

Habitat - A place where a certain organism lives.

Hardness - A property of minerals typically measured by comparing the mineral to ten minerals making up the Moh's Hardness Scale.

Heat - A property of energy usually measured as temperature.

Herbivore - Any animal that eats plants.

Humidity - The amount of water vapor in the air.

Hypothesis - An unproven scientific idea.

Igneous rock - Rocks formed when hot, liquid rock cools and hardens.

Infrared light - A region of the light spectrum of long wavelength light (7500 angstroms to about 1 millimeter).

Kenetic energy - The energy of motion.

Light - A type of radiation that may or may not be seen with the human eye.

Light spectrum - The visible wavelengths of light.

Luster - A property of mineral appearance such as metal-like, non-metal, clear, opaque, cloudy, dull.

Maria - Large areas of lava flow on the Moon.

Matter - Anything that occupies space and has mass.

Melange - An animal that has a biological parts that resemble other unrelated animals; e.g., the Australian platypus.

Meniscus - The concave depression made when water is in a column.

Metamorphosis - Changes that take place when an organism grows from larva to adult.

Metamorphic rock - Rock made when existing rock is changed by high heat and pressure.

Meteorite - A small to large piece of space rock entering the Earth's atmosphere.

Mineral - A single solid compound or element occurring by itself or with other minerals in rock.

Mitochondria - A small unit in the cell that contains a group of proteins called enzymes.

Monocotyledon - A seed type that is whole.

Nucleolus - A round body found within the nucleus of most cells.

Nucleus - A dense body, containing the cell's DNA.

Nutrient - Food for organisms.

Omnivore - An animal that eats both plants and animals.

Orbit - The path that a body makes in space as it moves around another body.

Osmosis - Transport of substances through a membrane.

Oxygen - The gas in air used by animals to breath.

Oxidize - The process of combining oxygen with substances.

Ozone - A gas in the upper atmosphere made up of three oxygen atoms. It has properties that protect Earth from ultraviolet light.

Paper Chromatography - A tool used by scientists to separate and identify substances in a mixture.

Perigee - The orbit of the Moon when it is closest to the Earth.

Periodic Table - A table containing all the elements organized according their properties.

Pollution - To add some harmful or potentially substance(s) to the environment or habitat.

Porosity - A measure of how fast water can flow through soil or rock.

Predator - An organism that captures live animals for food.

Pressure - The force caused by an object on another object.

Prey - An organism captured by a predator.

Radiation - The release and transfer of energy in wavelengths of light and heat.

Rock - A naturally form solid material usually formed from minerals.

Saturated - A solution cannot dissolve any more of a substance.

Sedimentary rock - Solid materials deposited by water, ice, or wind and cemented into rock.

Solar energy - Energy from the Sun.

Solution - A mixture of substances in a liquid.

Statistics - A branch of math used to study data.

Stem - The part of the plant supporting the leaves and containing the tissues transporting nutrients and water from the roots.

Stoma - A tiny opening or pore on the surface of a plant.

Stratosphere - The top layer of the atmosphere.

Sunspots - Magnetic storms on the surface of the Sun.

Survey - A method of collecting data that usually involves passive or uninvolved observation.

Taphonomy - The study of how fossils are made.

Tissues - Living material composed of various cells.

Transpiration - The loss of water vapor from the leaves and stems of plants.

Troposphere - The layer of the atmosphere closest to the Earth's surface.

Terrarium - A container habitat for plants and animals.

Vacuole - A hollow unit in the cell.

Vacuum - The absence of matter.

Weather - Changes in the atmosphere.

Work - The ability to cause change.

Xylem - Transport tissue in the plant.

NOTES

NOTES

NOTES